Library Management and Technical Services

The Changing Role
of Technical Services
in Library Organizations

Library Management and Technical Services

The Changing Role of Technical Services in Library Organizations

Jennifer Cargill
Editor

The Haworth Press
New York • London

Library Management and Technical Services: The Changing Role of Technical Services in Library Organizations has also been published as *Journal of Library Administration*, Volume 9, Number 1 1988.

The Haworth Press, Inc., 12 West 32 Street, New York, NY 10001
EUROSPAN/Haworth, 3 Henrietta Street, London WC2E 8LU England

Library of Congress Cataloging-in-Publication Data

Library management and technical services.

 Published also as v. 9, no. 1 of the Journal of library administration.
 Includes bibliographical references.
 1. Processing (Libraries)—Management. 2. Library administration. I. Cargill, Jennifer S.
Z688.5.L48 1988   025'.02   88-6824
ISBN 0-86656-779-8

Library Management and Technical Services

The Changing Role of Technical Services in Library Organizations

CONTENTS

Technical services have played an important, if unsung and often anonymous, role in the provision of library services since the beginning of the modern library. With the technologies introduced during the past twenty years, technical services have come to demand even more sophistication from the professionals practicing within that specialization of librarianship. Library services have benefitted extensively from the efforts of technical services librarians to adapt technological change to their environment. However, shortages in new librarians willing and interested in pursuing technical services careers threaten the trend of improved service promised by the continuing development of new automated systems and use of telecommunications.

Technical services operations are becoming more varied and complex. Automation, networking, and electronic information media are expanding capabilities and changing procedures. Barriers between traditional public and technical services departments are breaking down despite institutional inertia. Libraries, vendors, and networks are becoming more interdependent. Serials control is evolving as are serials themselves. Quality and authority control are more important than ever. Technical services librarians will face ever greater challenges requiring continuing education and development of new aptitudes. They will increasingly become database managers and providers of value-added services. Both public and academic libraries will come to resemble special libraries by providing such services.

Notable Literature of the 1980s for Technical Services

Gloriana St. Clair
Jane Treadwell
Vicki Baker

The literature of the 1980s is surveyed as a guide to engaging the problems of the 1990s. Citations are divided among automation, education, personnel management techniques, managing external constituents, and the role of technical services in the library. Proactive annotations reveal a concern with the future, rather than the past. Offerings from library and management literature guide librarians to greater efficiency and effectiveness. Technical services functions and organizational structure are analyzed as forces in the library change process.

ABOUT THE GUEST EDITOR

Jennifer Cargill, MSLS, MSEd, is Associate Director of Libraries for Information Access and Systems at Texas Tech University in Lubbock. She has published books and articles on a variety of topics within the library science field, and is a very active member of the American Library Association.

NEWS AND CALENDAR

For the past several months, library literature has been running heavy with stories on library education vs. library practice; the appropriateness of the graduate library degree; the ALA accredited degree vs. the non-ALA accredited degree; certification vs. degree requirements; and what libraries, librarians and library schools should be called assuming we should call them something else. In view of all the time and space being devoted to the identity and purpose of libraries/librarians, it may be time to get our act together if we expect anyone to take us seriously on any issue.

Leaders of the profession, in concert with the professional library organizations, may wish to lead a national debate on the topics of who we are, what we ought to be, and what we should be called. If for no other reason or goal than to affirm our current status and purpose, we must as a group of professionals determine among ourselves who and what we are before someone else does it for us. Library literature is also full of cases where others have made those decisions and the resulting consequences.

From an administrator's point of view, security is more than just making sure that doors and windows are locked or that the security exit is functioning properly. Security is in knowing and trusting the library staff and in being fully confident in delegating authority and responsibility for the most critical of operations. The library administrator and the personnel officer, through careful review and evaluation of application forms and contacts with former employers, can usually detect and avoid the problem applicant among a pool of applicants. Given all the care that goes into hiring a new employee, it is surprising and unfortunate, then, that relatively little attention is given to the employee, in terms of security matters, once that employee is on the job.

It seems that stories of library theft or embezzlement involving long-term or career librarians appear in library literature with greater frequency. Perhaps such problems are being reported more openly now and the problem itself is not on the increase. Still, the problem exists and will continue to exist due in part to the lack of adequate security procedures for physical facilities and checks and balances for fund accounting. Accountability for all library resources has been emphasized in recent years with the increased interest and emphasis on accountability at the institutional level. Governing boards, legislatures, and various organizations within higher education have made accountability a very high priority, and academic libraries in particular have been subjected to this closer scrutiny.

Security remains a problem, however, and the administrator in any type of library gets little assistance in this area. Consider the simple matter of custodial service in a library. How many times has your custodial crew been changed without your prior knowledge? What input do you have in selecting a new custodian? Does someone else choose your custodial staff for sensitive areas such as computer rooms, rare books collections, or areas where uncataloged books are kept? What security checks, if any, are made before a new custodian is placed in the library?

Consider also the potential security problems in those public libraries which serve as "host" to local residents who have violated a law or ordinance and must "serve time" in some civic capacity. Most offenders are guilty of minor errors in judgment and can indeed benefit from the experience of working in a library which serves the entire community. Other offenders have been charged with such offenses as driving under the influence or abuse of controlled substances.

Imagine, however, the fear, anger and general consternation felt by the staff of a public library known to this writer when it was discovered that a man convicted of highly publicized sex offenses was to be sentenced by the local judicial system to work off part of his punishment in the public library! There were few peaceful moments among the predominantly female staff while the man was "serving his time." In many cases, neither the director nor the library staff are informed of the nature of the offense committed by an individual, a fact which adds to the tension which is inevitable in such cases. To the administrator in particular, concern must range from the safety and welfare of the staff and patrons to the general security of the library. And heaven forbid should you violate the rights of the offender!

Another potential security problem, but one which encompasses very complex and often very painful human concerns, is the problem involving the chemically dependent employee. Recent library literature has carried reports on this topic and the damaging consequences, and no library administrator can safely assume that there will never be a problem with a chemically dependent employee. In addition to learning how to recognize signs of possible chemical dependency, the library administrator should be aware of the professional and legal ramifications of dealing with an alcoholic or drug addicted employee. By knowing your rights and responsibilities and the rights of the employee, potential problems can be more readily identified and resolved. A brief but pertinent introduction to the problems of working with a chemically dependent employee can be found in the Spring 1987 issue of *The Department Advisor*.

On an entirely different note, one of the more interesting developments in the library profession has surfaced in the form of a group of librarians who drafted and continue to refine the "We Are Not Pleased Manifesto." While the articles of the manifesto represent the collective views of just a few librarians at this time and may never be formally adopted by any library organization, many librarians could easily identify with and voice support for one or more of the articles. An interesting and healthy dialogue could result in widespread debate and action among the ALA membership. A draft of the manifesto, reviewed briefly in the August 1987 issue of *Library Journal*, was introduced during the San Francisco conference.

While reading through a backlog of mail, an article in *Higher Education & National Affairs* (Vol. 36, No. 13) caught my attention. The article, "Bill To Improve Research Facilities Endorsed," outlines a proposal called the University Research Facilities Revitalization Act of 1987 which was introduced by Robert A. Poe (D-NJ). If enacted and funded as planned, a sum of $250 million will be made available under the National Science Foundation to upgrade science laboratories and "other campus research facilities." There is no mention in the article concerning the eligibility of research libraries for the funds, and there are other sources of funds for libraries to enhance their collections and research potential. Nevertheless, research library directors should be alert to any opportunity to assist institutional leaders in applying for funds should the act be approved. Dollars from required matching funds and overhead costs could possibly find their way to the library as a necessary expenditure in upgrading the library's research potential, including materials and online capabilities, to match the upgrading of science labs and equipment.

San Antonio is behind us, and it is time once again to be thinking of the ALA Annual Conference to be held in New Orleans July 9-14, 1988. The weather will be a little different from that experienced last year in San Francisco, but conference participants will have no difficulty in finding challenging programs in all aspects of librarianship and, if one prefers, there should be little difficulty in finding things to amuse oneself between challenging programs.

Sydney, Australia will host the 1988 IFLA General Conference from August 30 through September 3. Attendees may wish to schedule some time for sightseeing away from the major cities. Back on this continent, the Public Library Association will meet in Pittsburgh April 27-30, 1988, and the Special Libraries Association will meet in Denver June 11-16, 1988. If it hasn't already passed, do something special during National Library Week (April 17-23). Perhaps you can give some thought to what you want to be called next year.

Coy L. Harmon

Introduction

THE CHANGING ROLE OF TECHNICAL SERVICES: WILL WE HELP TO CREATE THE FUTURE?

In recent years we have heard recurring complaints about the dearth of librarians trained and interested in the traditional technical services skills of acquisitions, cataloging, and serials. Is it completely a matter of a scarcity of librarians for these areas or is it also that libraries are changing and librarians have more career options to explore?

Technical services and its role in libraries is indeed changing. Librarians who might have pursued traditional, one-faceted careers are discovering that they can fill multifunctional positions where they can concentrate on using their professional talents in a combination of technical and public assignments. They have the option of becoming more involved in the interrelationships of different areas of libraries.

Librarians are also finding that there is a reexamination of the roles of professionals throughout libraries with more emphasis on librarians assuming managerial roles and totally professional responsibilities and paraprofessionals performing tasks that were until recently viewed as professional. Professional responsibilities are being redefined throughout libraries and especially in technical services.

For this collection, technical services librarians, technical services department heads, observers of technical services operations, vendor representatives, and administrators were asked to contribute their viewpoints on "The Changing Role of Technical Services." They have focused on technical services functions and organizational structure as forces within the library change process. Automation, personnel matters, education, management techniques, and

---

Jennifer Cargill is Associate Director of Libraries for Information Access and Systems at Texas Tech University, Lubbock, TX.

5

the role of technical services within the evolutionary library community are addressed. The focus is proactive. Many of the contributions are personal statements or opinion pieces, based on the authors' own experience as well as their research.

We will continue seeing technical services and libraries in general change as we also see library structures evolve. How technical services staff will participate in the change process will determine how those necessary technical skills remain a part of the rapidly changing structure of libraries.

Jennifer Cargill

Technical Services
in the Mission of the Library:
The "Back Room" Performers

Diane J. Cimbala

All but the most sophisticated library patrons are unaware that there are librarians and staff other than those at the reference and circulation desks; few have heard the terms "technical services" or "technical processing." Somehow materials are miraculously ordered, catalogued, and processed in preparation for access and circulation. Automated systems appear overnight and online public access catalogs are installed as easily as new television sets with VCRs. All librarians suffer from image and negative stereotype handicaps (not to mention low salaries), but technical services librarians and their staffs suffer under the worst burden of all: invisible anonymity!

In this essay on the role of technical services in the mission of the library, the author will review how the efforts of technical processing personnel have continuously enabled libraries to provide better, faster, more accurate access to information. How technological change has altered the work of technical processing librarians as well as the nature of library service will be addressed. New technologies have created opportunities to rethink existing organizational structures within libraries and their parent institutions and development of new job possibilities within those structures. However, only an informed user group will allow us to realize the extent of change that is possible and provide the library profession with a strong pool of applicants from which to attract new members.

The mission of most libraries is to provide information to their defined patron group. Information provision is multifaceted. Refer-

Diane J. Cimbala is Northeast Regional Representative for the F. W. Faxon Company's Academic Division.

ence librarians are crucial guides through the maze of books and other materials; they also serve an important role in teaching patrons how to take full advantage of the library's resources. The professionals who acquire, catalog, process, and create access to the information housed in the library are as crucial to its mission as the most helpful reference librarian. Unfortunately, we as technical services professionals have neglected to be our own advocates, and now face shortages of new librarians trained and interested in careers in the technical services. We are also faced with the challenge of conveying the importance of our work, and the systems available to do it with, to those who administer our institutions.

The technological changes that have shaped the traditional library profession over the past two decades have afforded dynamic members of the technical services fraternity the opportunity to create and sponsor change within their institutions. In most cases, the changes wrought have resulted in improved service for the end-user, both in terms of speed and accuracy. This trend can only continue, as new technologies force us to scrutinize existing organizational structures within the library itself, as well as those of parent institutions. More than automation itself, the proliferation of local area networks is expanding the scope and availability of library services, and is providing access to inhouse and commercial databases on a scale that was unimaginable just ten years ago. All librarians, but especially those in technical services functions, are developing new alliances with computer or data processing professionals within their institutions in order to ease the transition from paper to electronic communications, and from manual to automated systems. The library is gradually becoming a center of information not limited to the printed word, nor to the building with the word LIBRARY carved into its pediment.

The people behind this transition, however, are those most usually found in the back rooms or basements of the public and academic library: the cataloging, acquisitions, serials, and systems librarians, as well as technical services administrators. For the past 20 years, increasing numbers of these invisible professionals have been utilizing technologies to make information more accessible, accurate, and user-friendly. They have furthered and expanded the mission of the library—making it more than a repository for books and serials—converting it into an information center where data of all kinds is available, regardless of its form.

The most popular beginning step to improved access has been the installation and implementation of online circulation systems, which provide more accurate, efficient service as well as a current inventory of the status of library holdings. Librarians doing a brisk business in reserves have benefitted from the ability to provide faster, uniformly produced reserve lists and access that complements the library's regular circulating collection. From online circulation, many institutions look toward the creation of an online public access catalog which provides users with a multitude of searching and access options, as well as holdings information unmatched in currency by any other system. Many libraries have experimented with COM catalogs and CD-ROM technology to avail their users of a more portable system than the old card catalog. While still limited in currency, such systems enable libraries to distribute copies of their catalogs to their users, rather than forcing users to come to the library.

Now libraries are automating their acquisitions and serials control functions. Although the former rarely benefits the end-user in terms of access, the hastening of the ordering/payment process can provide faster, more accurate service than manual systems. *And* the automation of serials control can provide many of the same benefits inherent in online public access catalogs, particularly if the use of interfaces enables data transmission from serials checkin to the catalog holdings records. Automated serials systems, perhaps more than any other automated function, can also reduce the necessity for mindless clerical work and free staff time for more interesting, special projects. Most manual checkin systems require that the Kardex file be read on a regular basis to ensure that serial items are arriving in a timely fashion. Staff shortages make this task prohibitively time-consuming, and force libraries to take a reactive, rather than proactive, stance on claims. Vendor interfaces with integrated library systems can also eliminate the need to post invoice data manually into serials files, thus providing another major saving in staff time.

Undergirding each of the aforementioned functions is the core of technical processes: providing access to the library's own database through the generation of descriptive and bibliographic information in machine-readable form. We are able to create online catalogs, circulation and acquisitions systems because of the advent of bibliographic networks such as OCLC, RLIN, and WLN, and standards like LC-MARC. Without the introduction of data into such utilities, none of these other automated functional systems would be possible. Machine-readable bibliography has transformed the way the library is used. The responsibility of educating of users to automation falls on the public services staff, but without the efforts of technical services librarians there would be little to teach.

Now the advent of local and regional networks is creating even greater possibilities for the expansion of the library's mission and the definition of its geographic responsibilities. Many higher education institutions have implemented campus- or university system-wide networks on which a library's bibliographic database may be accessed and displayed. Some networks are expanding their menus to include access to online databases. Once again, it is incumbent upon the technical processes professionals to ensure that the library-generated data on such networks is complete and accurate.

Aside from bibliographic access, another function of technical services in supporting the library's mission is providing financial management. Within the realm of serials and monographic acquisitions falls the responsibility of selecting vendors and in some cases, the materials to be acquired, be they traditional library books and journals, or compact disks, videocassettes, films, software, or CD-ROM databases. The acquisitions librarians, in concert with their colleagues in cataloging, circulation and serials, often find themselves in the position to recommend investment in automated systems. They then pursue implementation, from writing the requests for proposal, to overseeing the proper installation of equipment, to effecting the transition from the manual system to the automated one. Automation projects can last several years, depending upon the size of the collection and the number of functions to be automated.

As of this writing, the fiscal responsibility of technical services departments is weighing even more heavily than in the early 1980s. Demographics, economics, and the current political climate have conspired to create an especially difficult time for academic and research libraries in particular. The falling dollar is stretching already tight materials budgets as foreign materials become almost unattainably priced, yet users have become accustomed to highly specialized collections containing current materials from international sources. Consequently, many librarians are scrutinizing their materials budgets and imploring their users (especially faculty and other researchers) and collection development officers to rethink their needs in terms of local library acquisitions. Any period of belt-tightening is likely to enhance the climate for resource-sharing, and once again, the value of the big bibliographic utilities, as well as other telecommunications networks, cannot be understated. Electronic mail systems facilitate communications, and there is increased discussion of the possibilities for electronic publishing of articles, if not monographs. Should electronic publishing become the norm, librarians in both public and technical services will be facing new questions regarding access to and retention of information.

Technological change has greatly affected librarians in the past two decades and will continue to do so for the next several decades. Through the 1980s the stated mission of the library has not altered dramatically, yet the means used to realize that mission have changed dramatically. As more and more information is available in machine-readable form librarians, particularly those in technical services, may find themselves redefining their jobs and educating themselves increasingly in the realm of systems. As we alter the definition of what constitutes "legitimate" library materials and implement increasingly sophisticated systems, the role of technical services librarians will gain even greater importance, while their distinction from data processing professionals will become decreasingly pronounced.

Other administrative questions arise with the advent of new technologies and their impact on the work of libraries. As the proliferation of bibliographic utilities eliminated the need for MLS-holding professionals to perform verification for interlibrary loans, or original cataloging for every item purchased for the collection, new systems will further alter the ways in which we use clerical staff as well as professionals. Traditional organizational structures should be scrutinized and each position reviewed to determine what level of education the work performed requires. At the same time, the public should be informed about the kinds of changes transforming the library and how those changes will affect access to information. Perhaps users would benefit from an understanding of the history behind these systems: what manual methods were like; why an automated system is preferred; who implements the systems; and what steps are taken to do so. A little public relations about the administrative and functional structure of the library might not only educate our patrons (and those who administer our parent institutions) but it could also upgrade our image and bring status to the profession.

One of the most critical responsibilities we now face is eliminating the shortage of new librarians who are prepared to address the technological changes wrought by the new information age. We need to make clear to new librarians that a career in technical services can prove to be challenging, dynamic, and even fun. Those of us who have already chosen careers in the "back room" need to make an effort to demonstrate the importance of our role to the overall mission of the library.

The Evolutionary Role
of Technical Services

James R. Dwyer

The stereotypical image of technical services is that of a background operation: low profile, reactive, almost exclusively task-oriented. Rapid developments in computer science and telecommunications are catalysts for change in technical services and provide greater opportunities for library employees to become proactive change agents.

Some scholars have posited the death of traditional libraries early in the next century. Libraries may indeed become anachronisms if they fail to respond effectively to a variety of challenges. Considering our relative success in obtaining, creating access to, and interpreting new media, the reported death of the library, to paraphrase Mark Twain, has been greatly exaggerated.

Public and academic libraries will survive because they fit the evolutionary model fairly well. They adapt to change and form symbiotic unions with other information and service providers. This isn't a true revolution, a sudden and radical shift in thinking, purposes, or methods, nor is it simply finding new ways of doing the same old things. In this century libraries have evolved from being primarily print repositories to providing audiovisual media, automation for circulation control and other inhouse tasks, networks for cataloging and resource sharing, online searching of remote databases, distributed processing, online catalogs, and new media such as online journals and CD-ROM. Technical services librarians have been active participants in all these developments and, in many cases, have provided leadership.

James R. Dwyer is Head of the Bibliographic Services Department at California State University, Chico, CA.

EVOLVING ROLES FOR TECHNICAL SERVICES

Technical Services is no longer a mere backstage operation — if it ever was. The work has become so central, multifaceted, and complex that it can't be considered mere "support services." The widespread acceptance of the MARC format as the language of library automation makes those fluent in it more than mere information packagers. As MARC-based systems are introduced to the library's public, technical services librarians interact more frequently with reference librarians and end users as interpreters of MARC-based records.

Librarians are increasingly called upon to help design and implement the very online systems they rely upon. These new systems then influence library operations. Thanks to distributed processing, libraries no longer need to be administratively organized around "our" files: the card catalog for cataloging, the Kardex for serials, the on order file for acquisitions, etc. As these files go online and become integrated or interfaced with other databases, the old barriers start to break down. Virtually all public and academic librarians today have a technical aspect to their job and almost all serve the public directly or indirectly.

The last two libraries at which this author has worked no longer use the terms Technical and Public Services. When asked "doesn't Bibliographic Services really mean Cataloging, and Collections Division really mean Technical Services?" I have to answer "Not really. That's the easy part of the job." The old terms have become inadequate. The new ones won't win any poetry contests, but they may be closer to the mark. In Bibliographic Services, for example, we are concerned not only with the contents of the online catalog but with its structure: parameterization, index manipulation, searching protocols, help screens, user documentation, etc. We also evaluate CD-ROM and other systems, perform collection development, lead tours, perform demos, work the reference desk, and teach classes. Yes, things have certainly changed. The boredom that was sometimes experienced as a cataloger has given way to stress. Ahh, progress.

In some cases, new names for positions or departments may be little more than window dressing but usually they indicate real reorganization and consequent shifts of responsibilities. Most libraries that have implemented or are planning for online systems have, at the very least, established multidepartmental committees to make recommendations. Such committees often set the stage for reorganization.

EVOLVING JOBS

Job titles may reflect formal credentials or roles rather than aptitudes and attitudes. We are no longer just clericals, paraprofessionals, or professionals. In the face of automation we become Wizards, Adepts, Copers, Hackers, Computer Wienies, or Phobes. Such titles won't appear on an organization chart but they reflect how the work actually gets done. In some situations there may be a rather weak correlation between position titles and technical competence. It must be noted, though, that organizational power moves toward those with the expertise to wield it effectively.

Data processing and communications are merging to create new information services. In addition to the traditional skills today's "compleat librarian" needs to understand the basics of hardware, software, applications, interfaces, networking telecommunications, and human information processing. Although they may lack detailed background in these areas, technical services librarians are noted for their attention to detail, concern for quality and accuracy, and knowledge of other standards. Anyone who can master AACR2 can certainly comprehend most computer manuals.

It is no longer unusual to find catalogers at the reference desk, acquisitions librarians at a computer console, or reference librarians working in cataloging or collection development. At Chico State, librarians are given a primary assignment in one department and a secondary assignment in another. Texas Tech University has created multifunctional Information Access Librarian positions such as Documents/Cataloging, Reference/Documents, or Acquisitions/Reference.

Institutions as diverse as Evergreen State College (as directed by Jim Holley, who might be called the "Mr. Natural" of Libraries) and the University of Illinois (under the late Hugh Atkinson) have attempted more "tribalized" structures with varying degrees of success. Holley has stated that he accepts no process as valid which intentionally or unintentionally leads to depersonalization at any level. A worthy goal, but difficult to attain.

PROBLEMS AND LIMITATIONS

The same factors that inhibit effective library operations can also create depersonalization. They include, but are not limited to, the following:

— Insufficient resources and poor salaries
— Restrictive job classification schemes
— Internal resistance to change
— Too much technical minutia
— Accountability

Insufficient resources (exacerbated by the curious notion that automation means less work) make it difficult to retain a large enough staff to carefully review records and enhance them, effectively develop collections, keep serials accessible and under control, incorporate new technologies, or staff the desks. In most libraries, public and technical services departments compete for scarce funds.

Restrictive classification schemes may be self-defeating. First, we call people clericals or paraprofessionals, implying that they need not have a professional attitude or service orientation. Then we package them in smaller numbered boxes of the "thou shalt not" variety. In the last decade much of the work previously done by librarians has been shifted to classified staff. Many local governments and universities audit positions according to how things have been done in the past rather than how they might be done better. For every successful position upgrade there are likely to be failures or even downgrades. (While one rarely reads about failures in the literature, failures can be discovered by keeping your ears open at conferences.)

Stifling personnel schemes are sometimes the result of collective bargaining. Although the author is almost always pro-union it is noticed that contracts intended to prevent exploitation often result in exploitation of a different kind: underemployment and low potential for advancement. A real multistep career ladder that actively promotes meritorious service, allows people to develop to their potential, and rewards them for it would be ideal. Unfortunately, low turnover and a tendency to classify positions at the lowest possible level is a more common scenario.

Internal resistance to change can be individual or institutional in nature. Some administrators may voice frustration that "our institutional metabolism" is too bureaucratic and slow to effectively respond to developments in the marketplace. The individual, on the other hand, may find the pace of change far too fast. (While preparing this paper the author routed a note to staff with a request to let him know what they thought about "The effect of online systems on your job." The responses? "They eat you alive!")

So how do we keep from being eaten alive by the computer? First, follow the good advice that "assumption is the mother of all screwup." Assume nothing and define terms carefully. Bring staff members into the planning and implementation of a system, not just for their sake, but for yours. You might have assumed something. Make them feel like they are an integral part of the organization and that they are partly responsible for the success or failure of the system. (They are whether you acknowledge it or not.) Provide training in advance and follow-up as required. Finally, periodically review implementation to determine whether the system, staff, and the library's policies and procedures are all pulling in the same direction. Even after all of that, people may still feel like computer fodder.

In nonlibrary videogames it's easy to see who is about to eat whom. OPACMAN is far trickier because the rules are so complicated, so infinitesimal, and change so often, that it is now a full-time job just to stay current with cataloging rules — especially LC interpretations — and developments in automation.

Accountability comes into question during times of organizational change. If you are assigned to more than one unit to whom do you report, who evaluates you, how do you set priorities and schedule your time? These are not trivial questions. The introduction of online systems implies that librarians must become fully interdependent if they wish to be truly effective. Interdependence can't be mandated and may be discouraged by traditional organizational models. Instead, it is something that develops over time as we work together toward mutual goals. If you have an automated system that works, you have something to be proud of and rally round. If you have a system that doesn't work, there's no unifier like a common enemy.

"WILL THE LAST CATALOGER PLEASE TURN OFF THE LIGHTS?"

One popular theme in library literature is "where have all the catalogers gone?" (The smart ones now work for a variety of cottage industries interpreting the interpretations!) Published accounts have maintained that the work is considered dull, deadended, and otherwise unrewarding, that cataloging is not promoted in library schools, that most cataloging is done by clerks, that feminism has opened up other jobs for women, and that students find special libraries more attractive than civic service or academe.

While these may (or may not) be valid explanations, consider two others. First is "The Lake Woebegone Complex" wherein "All the women are strong, all the men good looking, and all the catalogers are above average." Technical services was once considered a safe haven for introverts with weak oral or managerial aptitudes. Job announcements for catalogers now typically stress communication and management in addition to advanced degrees, computer expertise, etc. We are simply asking too much of entry level applicants and not assuming development of "people skills" on the job. A different factor that keeps more experienced workers away from cataloging is "cataloger bashing." All the little shortcuts and adaptations which are easily hidden in card catalogs are clear for all to see online. Who gets blamed for decades of shifts in policy, quick and dirty conversion projects, and past mistakes? Today's catalogers! We don't get no respect!

Cataloging, particularly subject analysis, can be very interesting work if one doesn't get too caught up in trivialities. Unfortunately, the stereotype of catalogers as nitpickers is largely validated by the complexities of post-AACR2 cataloging.

These complexities also create barriers to the merger of technical and public services. Speaking from painful experience, it's usually easier to train someone with a background in cataloging to work the desk than it is to teach a reference librarian to catalog. Realistic options include having reference librarians focusing on subject analysis or working in a single format. When in doubt, advise them to use the *Concise AACR2* and commonsense: "How might the public look for this? How can we help them?"

EVOLVING NETWORKS

Interdependence via networking has changed technical services operations. Accuracy and quality control become more important than ever in an online mode since small sins of commission or omission may make bibliographic records inaccessible. Although WLN insisted on quality and authority control from the beginning, the same cannot be said of the other bibliographic utilities. Over the last few years all utilities have made progress in quality control, partly through subnetworks of "master catalogers."

Shared databases, whether they take the form of national cataloging databases, union lists of serials, or shared local systems, demand a shared commitment to standards and a cooperative spirit. "Fear of cataloging" (not wanting other libraries to see your errors), "Let George do it" (waiting for someone else to catalog an item), "Quick and dirty" (rules, what rules?) and "What's in it for me?" (expecting networking to cut local costs and staff) are nemeses to effective networking.

The mere existence of networks has not introduced major costs savings, created equality among libraries, or led to massive resource sharing yet. Networks, like computers, are simply tools that have been adopted but not fully utilized in libraries. Public libraries have been significantly less active in networks than academic libraries for a variety of reasons: initial high investment, a perception of high continuing costs, and the self-fulfilling prophecy of public library administrators and boards that networks are most beneficial to academic libraries. Ironically, many public library systems operate as local resource sharing networks and the smallest libraries may have the most to gain from networking.

The shape of networking is becoming more complex. Some regional networks are primarily brokers for utilities while others offer a variety of products and services. The utilities have responded by offering CD-ROM cataloging modules, links to other databases, and products developed for reference librarians and end-users.

NETWORK TRENDS

One interesting trend is for libraries to serve as subcontractors for vendors or networks. A few examples include OCLC members providing cataloging copy for major microform sets or enhancing and upgrading records: Rice, Texas A & M, and Louisiana State University Libraries cleaning up GPO records for MARCIVE; and libraries serving as test sites for systems or software still in development. Such projects are commendable, but very demanding. The initial workload perception is often just the tip of the iceberg and the project may take years to complete.

Another trend is the appearance of new sources of machine-readable records. Just as traditional vendors such as H.W. Wilson provided catalog cards in competition with the Library of Congress Card Distribution Service, vendors now compete with utilities and online services for their own share of the cataloging and indexing market. Electronic analogs to catalog cards and printed indexes (such as Bibliofile, InfoTrak, BIP Plus or a host of ERIC-based products) have gained rapid popularity in both academic and public libraries.

Local networks and reorganizations are also becoming more commonplace. Online catalogs in public libraries sometimes refer patrons directly to other community agencies. Pikes Peak Library District's "Maggie's Place" serves as a fine example. Academic libraries increasingly cooperate with campus computer centers and are sometimes jointly administered, e.g., Columbia University, California State University-Chico, and California State University-Long Beach. Public libraries often share time on a city or county computer.

Information networks even exist within libraries. A decade ago it was popular to say that "online catalogs should include everything." Given limited system capacity, different searching protocols, different information, and even different purposes of various files, interfacing usually makes more sense than total integration. The patron would like to move among cataloging, acquisitions, serials, other local databases, and external files as seamlessly as possible. This places a greater burden on librarians to develop easy linkages and provide ever more sophisticated training.

PROLIFERATION OF SERIALS

Due to their price, proliferation, popularity, changing titles, cessations, and splits, serial publications have posed a special challenge to technical services operations. They sometimes seem to resemble a bottomless pit, devouring an ever larger percentage of the budget, staff, and space. Acquisitions and serials control systems are becoming more complex and powerful and hold out some hope for better and less costly operations in the future by integrating a variety of functions such as subscriptions, bookkeeping, claiming, and binding. Beware that the transition from manual to automated systems can be slow and costly! Such transitions almost inevitable lead to changes in a variety of policies and procedures and can be a catalyst for reorganization.

Online publishing poses further challenges. While the print format is stable in terms of the content of individual issues, electronically stored files can be for more volatile and might even allow interaction with users. Likely developments include merging text and index files, storing and unbundling articles electronically (you don't "own the magazine," but can download and copy!), and ever more specialized information services. Given the popularity of print periodicals, they are unlikely to go the way of the eight-track tape or Screaming Yellow Zonkers. Scholarly journals are likelier candidates for exclusively electronic form.

CRISES OF RAISED EXPECTATIONS

Thanks to overselling the power of automation while understating its limitations, several crises of raised expectations have emerged. Librarians demand the sun and moon. Vendors promise the whole galaxy and typically deliver an asteroid belt for library staff to reassemble. Ever more sophisticated users demand "blue sky" features that we can't yet provide. Technical services is dependent on the vendor to make such improvements so staff may justifiably feel "stuck in the middle."

Consider the global fix. First libraries said they needed not only keyword searching but browsing of existing headings with rigorous authority control. The vendors responded with the "global fix" whereby all records containing a heading can be changed simultaneously. For as long as a decade some libraries have minimized their item-by-item approach to authority control while waiting for the global fix—but that's like waiting for Godot. In the meantime, online catalog users are surprised to find that you have few, if any, of Mark Twain's books in the library. They may even go to Interlibrary Loan or a different library to find materials in their local library's collection.

Consider the scholar's workstation providing an online catalog, access to other databases, downloading of text and citations, word processing, spreadsheet, and database management software. Such a project was attempted at Brown University and failed because the expectations of faculty developed faster than the system's capabilities and the time and cost to develop it were underestimated. The new products from Personal Bibliographic Software and some other vendors are more modest in their claims and more effective. Research continues on more advanced workstations and on artificial intelligence, but it is too soon to predict what effect they may have on library technical services. Just as dumb terminals are often replaced with microcomputers, we can expect those micros to form the basis of increasingly complex workstations.

Consider the linking of automated systems which operate in real-time to manual processes which don't. Including acquisitions, serials checkin, and bindery information in the online catalog inevitably puts more pressure on acquisitions and cataloging to produce the desired item — not when we are done cataloging, or binding, or physically processing it, but NOW! Using automation without a thorough assessment of its impact and appropriate changes in policies and procedures can be hazardous to your health. You know you are on the cutting edge of technology when you have the blood to prove it. Frustrating as raised expectations may be, though, they can help show the path to future improvements.

QUALITY CONTROL

A library is only as good as the information it provides. A system is only as good as the database it operates upon. Networks and online services allow a patron to access information not only available in, but through their local library. A library can hope to meet the increasingly sophisticated demands placed upon it through access to more and better databases.

Production or performance can no longer be judged in purely quantitative terms such as units cataloged, issues checked in, articles copied, or reference questions answered. Quickly converting those 600,000 books a few years back doesn't seem to be such an accomplishment when typos, incorrect tagging, and incomplete information preclude effective searching.

Quality control is essential. The first step is cleaning up records and providing effective authority control. To this end, some libraries have established bibliographic database manager positions, or even entire departments. The next step is enhancing those records with contents notes, summaries or scope notes when appropriate, and locally relevant subjects and added entries. Does your clientele like to read historical or biographical fiction? Then add subject headings to those records. Are they fluent in buzzwords as opposed to LCSHese? Then add keyword-rich notes and/or locally generated cross references. Just because we may be committed to the MARC format doesn't mean we can't use it more creatively and effectively. We need to teach our systems to speak the vernacular, not obtuse "infosci" jargon. Over time, the capabilities of online catalogs will encourage librarians to provide access at the micro-level (articles, papers, sections of books, tiny subsets of databases) through enhanced records and links between online catalogs and indexes.

Such enhancements are only possible through the intervention of skilled library workers who are familiar with both the public they serve and advances in library and information science. This implies that we will continue to require professionals in technical services positions and that we must provide deeper training for support staff. It does not imply that any given type of organization is best for all libraries or that technical or public services be totally merged. Ask what will work in your library to provide the best service and be willing to experiment with different models—but never change just to be trendy.

A decade ago you could say "Here's the card catalog; here are the printed indexes; and there's where we do online searching." Different tools, different and relatively simple jobs for librarians, but pity the poor user who has to run from the indexes to the catalog to the serials list to the current periodicals desk, to the Kardex, etc. We will continue to have printed and online tools, but more indexes are going online (or on CD-ROM) and more databases are being linked, offering the potential for more effective use.

TECHNICAL SERVICES IS DEAD.
BRING ON THE COMPUTER CLOWNS.
LONG LIVE TECHNICAL SERVICES.

That brings us to the concept of "the technical services librarian as database manager." Consider this scenario:

Early to mid-1970s—Bibliographic utilities come into their own. Loss of some professional cataloging positions, lack of adherence to standards, and conversion projects focusing on quick production lead to degraded records and minimal subject access.

Late 1970s to early 1980s—Conversion to AACR2 forms without functional online authority creates considerable confusion.

Mid-1980s — "Why can't I find this in the online catalog? I know you have it?" leads to stronger commitment to standards and raises the status of tech services librarians to a degree. They often find themselves "training the trainers."

Late 1980s — Newer information "packages" such as CD-ROM, nonbibliographic databases, electronic journals, etc. become more prevalent in and out of libraries.

Early to mid-1990s — The Acquisitions, Catalog, and Serials librarians who have been working both with systems and the public are now well on their way to becoming database managers capable of selecting, interfacing, and evaluating a variety of electronic and print information sources and offering value-added services through public workstations and home terminals. RTSD and RASD disappear because LITA meetings are so much more interesting.

By the year 2000 — many academic and public librarians fill roles very similar to what many special librarians do today: not just locate sources but they deliver the actual information along with recommendations. Some will serve as "vertical" subject specialists and others as "horizontal" generalists. The term "technical services" will have become obsolete, but the work done in today's technical services departments will be done better than ever under a variety of organizations appropriate to individual libraries. Information resources will be almost seamlessly interfaced so that the public has direct, timely, and effective access to what it needs to know. The status of librarians rises to the point where an actual librarian becomes Librarian of Congress.

Is this too rosy a picture? Quite possibly. What will happen to small libraries who lack initial automation funds and varied staff expertise? What about funding for publicly supported libraries? Will our greying profession keep up with and even lead the way to new developments or will we suffer from increased stress and future shock? Can we attract an infusion of new, first-rate talent? Will leaner information brokerage firms capable of quicker change supplant libraries to a large degree? Is the library's share of the total information market too small for us to help "shape the future?"

Questions about the evolutionary role of technical services are inevitably couched in larger questions about the future of the profession. Our ability to proactively identify and respond to such challenges will determine our success.

BIBLIOGRAPHY

A Selection of Recent (1984-87) Articles and Books

Allen, Geoffrey G. "Change in the Catalog in the Context of Library Management." *Journal of Academic Librarianship* 12 (July 1986):141-3.

Alley, Brian. "A Conversation with Hugh Atkinson." *Technicalities* 5 (April 1985):3-7.

Atkinson, Hugh C. "Atkinson on Networks." *American Libraries* 18 (June 1987):432-9.

Aveney, Brian. "Electronic Transmission in Acquisitions Systems." *Technical Services Quarterly* 2 (Spring-Summer 1985):17-31.

Bland, Robert. "Quality Control in a Shared Online Catalog Database: The Lambda Experience." *Technical Services Quarterly* 4 (Winter 1986):43-58.

Bryant, Bonita. "The Organizational Structure of Collection Development." *Library Resources & Technical Services* 31 (April-June 1987):111-22.

Burke, Marianne. "Catalog Tectonics: Reflections on New Technology and Cataloging." *Technicalities* 7 (January 1987):3-4.

Busch, Joe. "Coming Out of the Back Room: Management Issues for Technical Services in the Eighties." *Technical Services Quarterly* 2 (Spring-Summer 1985):115-41.

Crismond, Linda. "The Future of Public Library Services." *Library Journal* 111 (November 15, 1986):42-9.

Dwyer, James R. "The Computer Mystique and the Librarian's Image." *Technicalities* 6 (October 1986): 1, 15.

———. "Evolving Serials, Evolving Access: Bibliographic Control of Serial Literature." *Serials Review* 2 (Summer-Fall 1986):59-64.

Fayen, Emily Gallup. "Beyond Technology: Rethinking 'Librarian.'" *American Libraries* 17 (April 1986): 240-2.

Freedman, Maurice J. "Automation and the Future of Technical Services." *Library Journal* 109 (June 15, 1984):1197-1203.

Godden, Irene P., ed. *Library Technical Services: Operations and Management.* Orlando, FL: Academic Press, 1984.

Gorman, Michael. "Dealing with Serials: A Sketch of Contextual/Organizational Response." *Serials Librarian* 10(Fall-Winter 1986):13-18.

———. "Laying Siege to the 'Fortress Library.'" *American Libraries* 17 (May 1986):325-8.

Hafter, Ruth. *Academic Librarians and Cataloging Network: Visibility, Quality Control, and Professional Status.* Westport, CT: Greenwood Press, 1986.

———. "Born-Again Cataloging in the Online Networks." *College & Research Libraries* 47 (July 1986):360-4.

Harrington, Sue Ann. "The Changing Environment in Technical Services." *Technical Services Quarterly* 4 (Winter 1986):7-19.

Hill, Janet Swan. "Wanted: Good Catalogers." *American Libraries* 16 (November 1985):728-30.

Horny, Karen L. "Fifteen Years of Automation: Evolution of Technical Services Staffing." *Library Resources & Technical Services* 31 (January-March 1987):69-76.

_____. "New Turns for a New Century: Library Services in the Information Age." *Library Resources & Technical Services* 31 (January-March 1987):6-11.

_____. "Quality Work, Quality Control in Technical Services." *Journal of Academic Librarianship* 11 (September 1985):206-10.

Intner, Sheila S. "Interfaces." *Technicalities* (column, 1986).

Presley, Roger L., and Robison, Carolyn L. "Changing Roles of Support Staff in an Online Environment." *Technical Services Quarterly* 4 (Fall 1986):25-39.

Presley, Roger L. "The Goldfish Bowl Effect of an Online Serials Control System." *Serials Librarian* 11 (December-January 1987):101-9.

Rocke, Hans J., and Ross, Johanna C. "Online Catalogs for and by Librarians." *Technical Services Quarterly* 2 (Spring-Summer 1985):1-10.

Ryan, Frederick, and Sessions, Judith. "Converging Technologies in California." *Wilson Library Bulletin* 61 (June 1987):16-20.

Schuman, Patricia Glass. "Library Networks: A Means, Not an End." *Library Journal* 112 (February 1, 1987):33-7.

Smith, Laurie E. "Where are the Entry Level Catalogers?" *Journal of Library Administration* 6 (Summer 1985):33-35.

Turock, Betty J., and Turock, David L. "An Investigation of Public Library Participation in Bibliographic Networks." *Library Resources & Technical Services* 31 (January-March 1987):35-59.

White, Herbert S. "Catalogers: Yesterday, Today, Tomorrow." *Library Journal* 112 (April 1, 1987):48-9.

Leadership versus Management
in Technical Services

Donald E. Riggs

Technical services have always included some of the most complex activities in libraries. Technology and more sophisticated personnel practices have contributed little toward simplifying technical services. The changing environment in this area of the library poses a challenge for those librarians who are responsible for planning the technical services future and making it happen. The implementation of AACR2 is a good example of a challenge that found many libraries unprepared to handle. Closing the card catalog and automating serials are other examples of projects that caught technical services managers off guard.

Tauber defined technical services as "services involving the operations and techniques for acquiring, recording, and preserving materials."[1] This definition remains applicable to today's composition of technical services. In some settings, collection development responsibilities have been removed from technical services, and circulation functions have been added to technical services. The complexities and challenges remain, notwithstanding the few changes in technical services. "Exactness," "production driven," "task oriented," and "high cerebral" are some adjectives commonly used to describe the work performed in technical services.

Prior to the introduction of modern technology to operations and procedures, only a few library science students expressed an interest in technical services. Reference services tended to be a favorite area for the holder of the freshly-minted MLS. It was not uncommon to hear these entry-level librarians say that they did not want to go in to technical services because the work was too demanding, too much "clerical-like," and too boring. In the late 1970s a library

Donald E. Riggs is University Librarian at Arizona State University, Tempe, AZ.

would receive three times as many applications for a vacant reference position as it would for a vacant cataloger position. However, there has been a turn in this employment interest to where the applications for reference and cataloging positions are similar in number.

Technology is definitely a determining factor in this renewed interest in technical services. Moreover, a different type of leader providing strategic direction has made technical services work more exciting. This new breed of technical services leader has provided vision, zeal, and fervor. It is very important to keep production levels high, manage the day-to-day operations in an highly efficient manner, and maintain orderly processes, *but* it is more important for the head of technical services to be a leader. Leadership begins where management ends.

DIFFERENT BOUGHS ON SAME TREE

Naturally, technical services require someone who can take charge and be responsible for getting the work done. Increasing and sustaining productivity is a responsibility that cannot be slighted. Excellent management of technical services realizes results, and results get attention. Services throughout the library are enhanced when technical operations, processing, and techniques are performed in the most efficient manner. Management and Leadership belong on the same tree, but they have to be recognized as different boughs. Bennis and Nanus in *Leaders* describe the difference between leadership and management:

> The problem with many organizations, and especially the ones that are failing, is that they tend to be overmanaged and underled. They may excel in the ability to handle the daily routine, yet never question whether the routine should be done at all. There is a profound difference between management and leadership, and both are important. "To manage" means "to bring about, to accomplish, to have charge of or responsibility for, to conduct." "Leading" is "influencing, guiding in direction, course, action, opinion." The distinction is crucial. *Managers are people who do things right* and *leaders are people who do the right thing*. The difference may be summarized as activities of vision and judgment—*effectiveness* versus activities of mastering routines—*efficiency*.[2]

It is believed by some that by simply walking through a library's technical services area, one can detect whether the head of technical services is a leader or a manager. This approach to determining leadership is an oversimplification. An observation of physical arrangement of work areas, installation of modern technology, and the general appearance of technical services is not the way to determine leadership effectiveness. Such an observation may reflect well on management acumen only. The essence of leadership is people. Further, all leadership capacities in technical services are not vested in the head of the technical services division. Department heads (e.g., head of acquisitions) must be recognized as leaders in the division. Leadership over human beings is exercised when motives and purposes mobilize institutional, political, psychological and other resources so as to arouse, engage and satisfy the motives of followers.[3]

TRANSFORMATIVE DIRECTION

Technical services have experienced a major transformation during the past decade. These drastic changes have occurred as a result of both happenstance and design. The implementation of modern technology in technical services has created many changes, and more technological advances can be expected in the future. Managers perform many transactional roles; they are good at seeing that the important day-to-day activities in technical services are completed. Transactional managers take pride in leaving work each day with a clean desk. Every organization needs transactional managers.

A notch above the transactional manager is the transformational leader. This person is creative, possesses "high-octane" energy, and recruits a library staff who reflects an optimum service philosophy. This type of leader enjoys making things happen. A transformative direction is established; changes are made in the way things are done. Professional and support staff in technical services become more confident in their work toward attainment of the division's goals and objectives. The staff's perspective moves from a mechanistic view (direct cause and effect) to an organic view (multiple causes and effects). The transformative direction encourages staff to engage in more innovative levels of technical service activities; there is a movement from task motivation to people-interaction motivation. Targets of opportunity are pounced upon by technical services; new strategies and collective energies are pulled together toward the attainment of agreed-upon goals/objectives. These collective aspirations are achieved as a result of the symbiotic relationship between the leaders in technical services and their followers.

PROBLEM FINDERS

One of the most vital things a leader can do for technical services is instilling a new mind state about thinking why processes and techniques need to be completed, why they are performed in the current manner, and why it may be better to do them another way. This type of "critical thinking" places "know-why" ahead of "know how." Managers deal with the "know how" aspects of technical services. Very few managers spend much time thinking about the philosophical basis for having a technical services function in the library. Leaders, on the other hand, fully understand and can articulate why the technical services function is important to the entire fabric of the library and to the library's parent institution. Bennis believes leaders have to look inward as well as forward:

> If a leader is not careful, he will be sucked into spending all his time on the important but stifling and inevitably mundane tasks of organizational maintenance. Leadership is the capacity to infuse new values and goals into the organization, to provide perspective on events and environments which, if unnoticed, can impose constraints on the institutions. . . . Administration is managing given resources efficiently for a given mission. Leaders question the mission. Once the leader gets sucked into the incredibly strong undertow of routine work, he is no longer leading, he is following, which he is not paid to do.[4]

Managing by Wandering Around (MBWA) is described by Peters and Austin as the technology of the obvious.[5] MBWA gleans for the leader the concerns of the staff at all levels throughout technical services. The basic intent of MBWA is to keep in touch with what is happening across all technical services' fronts. Leaders in technical services should talk with staff outside of the division to see what concerns/perceptions abound about the products and services of the division. Such discussions can occur without circumventing other authorities in the library construct. The feedback from these discussions should benefit the entire library.

Routine problem solving is the responsibility of the manager. Anticipating problems and their solutions is the role of the technical services leader. Thus, it is crucial for the technical services leader to know the heartbeat of the division, to seek out problems, and to critically think through solutions to problems.

POWER

We do not hear the word "power" being discussed by librarians; it is seldom, if ever, carried as a program topic at library conferences, and no one writes about it in the library literature. Why? Perhaps one reason is that library leaders do not want to show any signs of flaunting their power. However, modesty by this group should not curtail discussion and investigation of power in libraries by others interested in the topic. Ironically, we all have a thirst for more outstanding leaders in the profession while concurrently not taking the time to develop a better understanding of the use of power. Librarianship is not alone in its suppression of "power" and "authority." Other professions and the American people at large have turned their backs to the concept of power. However, these same people have a hunger for compelling and creative leadership. It is impossible to have strong leaders who have no power. Is there anything worse than a "powerless" leader? We have failed to recognize that the nucleus of leadership is power. Power is not a process designed to hurt someone, and it should not be perceived as being hostile. Power is not designed to lead to corruption, deceit, cruelty, and insensitivity. To the contrary, power is the essential energy to translate intention into reality. It is merely the ability to make decisions, engage in risk taking, and to make things happen.

Leaders cannot lead without power. This basic energy is necessary for initiating and sustaining action. Technical services leaders cannot make things happen without power. The head librarian has to delegate power to the head of technical services, and in turn the department heads must have appropriate power delegated to them. Ideally, the technical services staff will understand and appreciate the constructive uses of power. Power is the most necessary but most distrusted part of leadership.

VISION

Leadership implies that the holder is visionary, to paraphrase Shelley, to see the present in the past and the future in the present. It is incumbent on the head of technical services to create a vision of success and mobilize the division's employees to align behind that vision. This vision must be reflected in the mission statement for technical services. The head of the division and heads of the departments should collectively create visions of potential opportunities for technical services. Brainstorming in group sessions is an excellent way for identifying windows of opportunities. The "multiple futures" approach will assist participants in projecting what technical services "would like to be," and "is likely to be," and it provides a forum for concentrating on an "extreme contrast" case. Some of the greatest insights may occur from the projection of an extreme contrast of what technical services is likely to be in the future. Formulating alternative futures allows the freewheeling necessary for intellectual glimpses into potential futures. If only a figment of the "real" future of technical services can be envisioned through these exercises, they are worth the effort. Sharing visions of technical services' future will be advantageous and will likely pull the division together as it develops a focused enterprise.

Developing a vision for technical services is not enough. The leaders must also know how to harness the vision and to bring it to fruition. The vision must be realistic, credible, and one that is supported by a consensus within technical services. When the technical services vision of the desired future is established, professional and support staff in the division are able to find their roles not only in the division but also in the library. Staff at all levels in the division will bring greater enthusiasm to their positions when they know that the division has made a commitment to a focused future. People like to participate in designing a future with a purpose and direction, and due to their "buy in" with the endeavor, they will commit energies to bring desired intentions into reality.

PLANNING

Vision precedes planning. Without a vision, planning is nearly impossible. Before planning can actually take place, a vision has to animate, transform, and inspirit purpose into action. Vision deals with emotions, values, aspirations, and other nontangible matters, while planning focuses on more tangible issues; in short, planning is geared more to reality.

Now is an exciting time to engage in planning the future of technical services. However, traditional planning will not suffice. The continual changes being made in technical services demand a planning process that is ongoing and being updated at least annually. Strategic planning is the best planning process for technical services. Strategic planning does not focus principally on daily operations or budgetary issues. It does deal with broad intentions of the library; it serves as a planning process which analyzes future threats and opportunities, and it offers alternative courses of action for the library's consideration.[6] One of the best rewards for engaging in strategic planning is that it enables technical services to critically look at current practices and to ask questions such as:

1. What is the existing situation of technical services?
2. What is desired in the future for technical services?
3. What might inhibit the desired future of technical services?
4. What actions should be taken to achieve the goals and objectives of technical services?

The concept of strategic planning is powerful. Strategic planning solely for the sake of engaging in this type of planning process is not desirable. The true value of strategic planning is in the thinking it promotes in the technical services' personnel involved in the process and its implementation. Undoubtedly, strategic planning requires more cerebral activity than any other planning technique. Davis describes the "thinking" aspect of strategic planning as follows:

> In the placid world of traditional librarianship, strategic thinking was an unnecessary and indeed alien idea connoting conniving in its worst extreme. The library was meant to be carried wherever the satisfaction of the user needs took it. In the turbulent, resource scarce environment of contemporary librarianship, strategic thinking becomes indispensable. However, most librarians are simply not practiced in strategic thinking, which requires a shift in mind set. A mind which is used to thinking forward from action to consequences, must begin to focus on "backward analysis" from desirable future outcomes to immediate requirements. Capability to think stra-

tegically needs to be developed in most managers; unfortunately, it seldom is.[7]

Leaders, rather than managers, prefer strategic planning because the development and implementation of strategies is the backbone of strategic planning. Formation of strategies requires brainstorming and thinking. The strategy-formation activity is never-ending; strategists must keep in tune with new developments impacting technical services and they have to consciously design and regularly assess each strategy.

The strategic plan developed for technical services must be in conformance with the strategic plan for the library. If the library does not have a strategic plan, technical services could develop its own plan. However, it may be a bit awkward to get the support of the head librarian for a localized strategic plan. Assuming that the library has a strategic plan, the first step is to get the technical services strategic plan in sync with the overall library plan. The mission statement for technical services is to support the mission statement for the entire library system. After the mission statement is refined, goals and objectives are established; strategies are formulated for the goals and objectives. Leaders in technical services will find it very prudent to see that individual staff members' annual goals are closely related to the strategic plan's goals/objectives.

Technological advances will continue to have a measurable impact on technical services. The burden is on technical services leaders to put technology in the proper perspective. Technology is not an end; it is a means to an end. Those who operate in the inactive or reactive mode while dealing with new technologies will end up as "strategic failures."

THE ENTREPRENEURIAL LEADER

It is no secret that entrepreneurism is in vogue. Today, entrepreneurs are hailed as the strength of our country, the hope of the future, the affirmation of our ideals, the cat's meow. Granted, most of the entrepreneurial activities are taking place in the private and corporate world. Nevertheless, the library world most certainly needs an injection of the entrepreneurial spirit.

The entrepreneurial leader in technical services is best described as one who is an innovator, a creative person, and one who dislikes maintaining the status quo. Unquestionably, the entrepreneur wants to see results immediately. It is best to judge the entrepreneur on attainment of goals/objectives, and not on the process used to achieve the desired output. Very few library managers can be classed as entrepreneurs; this class is reserved for leaders. Managers tend to like things nice and tidy. An entrepreneurial leader in technical services may generate some discomfort among colleagues. An entrepreneur will have the effect of challenging old norms in technical services, something not always looked upon favorably. Some people in technical services may feel threatened by an entrepreneurial leader, mainly because they are most secure in their positions when things are quiet and are made uneasy within a changing environment. The entrepreneurial leader must be sensitive to the discomfort of those who have long resisted any change in technical services' operations and techniques. The change maker should never attack colleagues when challenging a technical services activity; the attack should be upon inflexible objectives, ideas, or procedures. The typical entrepreneur is a tough, competitive risk taker with a firm conviction to succeed. Entrepreneurs may be risk takers, but they are not gamblers. They are calculated risk takers; their risk taking occurs in areas over which they have control, and where their planning and projections can offer some hedge against unpredictable future. Technical services, as other areas of the library, need persons with entrepreneurial attributes. If there is a major reservation about entrepreneurial leaders, it is that they like to do things themselves rather than work through their colleagues. In the corporate world entrepreneurs tend to work independently. Only time will tell how effective an entrepreneurial leader can serve in the library arena.

POSITIVE SELF-REGARD

Leadership is a deeply personal business. The higher one goes in leadership positions, the more interpersonal and human one's work becomes. Executives in Fortune 500 firms spend roughly 90 percent of their time with others. These same executives must pay close attention to managing themselves; the use of their time is vital to their effectiveness. Leaders in technical services are very similar to these high-level executives in many ways. They, too, must first be able to manage themselves before they can manage and lead their colleagues.

In their study of various leaders in all walks of life, Bennis and

Nanus found no trace of self-worship or cockiness; they also arrived at the following definition of what positive self-regard is not: "To begin with, it is not a crowing self-importance or egotistic self-centeredness. . . . Nor is it what's ordinarily meant by a 'narcissistic character.'"[8]

Leaders must have self-respect. They have to believe in their abilities. The self-evolving leaders are those who recognize their strengths and compensate for their weaknesses. It is unwise for any technical services leader to assume universal knowledge of all areas of technical services.

Leaders with positive self-regard interact with others in the following ways:

1. The ability to accept people as they are, not as you would like them to be.
2. The capacity to approach relationships and problems in terms of the present rather than the past.
3. The ability to treat those who are close to you with the same courteous attention that you extend to strangers and casual acquaintances.
4. The ability to trust others, even if the risk seems great.
5. The ability to do without constant approval and recognition from others.[9]

COMPASSION

Effective leaders are compassionate people. They genuinely care about their followers. Technical services leaders will readily see signs of better morale, increased productivity, and more collaborative efforts if colleagues are treated with compassion. Needless to say, the staff is the most precious resource of any library division/department. Library leaders should make an extra effort to formulate goals that will bring out the very best in the staff. Douglas McGregor's Theory Y—the integration of individual and organizational goals—should be in every library leader's repertoire.

Compassion is somewhat like power. Very little is written about it, and it also never appears as a topic on a library conference program. Why? Are library leaders afraid to let their guard down and openly admit that they really care about their staffs? The "distance" between the supervisor and subordinate can be maintained in technical services while at the same time treating subordinates in the most humane manner possible. Mutual respect will develop between leaders and followers in such an environment and there will be little or no overfamiliarity issues. The ability to let another working colleague know that the leader of the division/department really cares about the individual and appreciates one's contributions is an important element of effective leadership.

STAFF DEVELOPMENT

Leaders, more than managers, will be more attuned to the imperfections of the technical services staff. Leadership is responsible for developing and refining a more desirable future for followership. With the emphasis on exactness in much of technical services' activities, the comment that "If you haven't ever made a mistake, you haven't been trying hard enough" is appropriate while addressing staff development. A good leader is one who stretches the staff to do more in order to achieve lofty goals. Provision must be made for embracing errors and engaging in calculated risk taking. Leaders have to strive for a fit between the strengths of technical services staff and the established organizational requirements for the division.

Technical services is one of the more dynamic areas in the library. Staffing requirements keep changing to meet the new demands. The online environment has forced modifications in job descriptions. Working with an online public catalog in lieu of the card catalog has necessitated a new approach to catalog maintenance. New technology in serials control has resulted in long-awaited streamlining of procedures. These are only a few changes that have made it necessary for professional and support staff to upgrade their skills or retool for new responsibilities and duties. Leaders in technical services are cognizant of these changes and most are taking the initiative to provide a positive environment for coping with new staff development requirements.

In library circles technical services personnel are held more accountable for sustaining high production levels than personnel in most other library divisions. This expectation has its pros and cons. On the positive side, after a day's work one can reflect proudly on what was accomplished. We all like to see measurable results of our efforts. On the other side, one cannot keep production up at the highest levels if there is an expectation that one should participate in workshops, conferences, and other programs that will update or improve technical services' skills. Understanding leaders will make allowances for participation in these necessary programs. They are aware of the fact that enhancing the skills of staff is a sound investment for the division/department. In addition to making time for program attendance, it is wise for leaders in technical services to allow the professional staff release time per week (e.g., 10 percent) to work on relevant projects. Projects of this nature must have the blessing of the immediate supervisor. Time will reflect that these programs and projects will result in better technical services. Staff will have an improved sense of worth, be more energized, and enjoy a stronger commitment to the division's mission.

MOTIVATE AND INSPIRE

Theory X — motivating by the carrot-and-stick way — no longer works. People want something more meaningful than a few tangible rewards. Improvement in the workplace has always been a high priority for workers in virtually all types of employment. Followers like to know what the intentions of leaders are and appreciate learning about these intentions through direct and concise communication from leaders. Communication is an important responsibility of leaders, and it can be used as a motivating force if the leaders transmit their interpretations and meanings of desired outcomes in such a way that followers feel they are part of the action. Followers must enjoy a true sense of worth in technical services. The leader can motivate and inspire followers by articulating and embodying the ideals toward which technical services are striving. "Striving for excellence" is an appropriate theme for any organization to follow. A theme of this nature inherently develops a "win-win" perspective for all persons associated with the organization. Values shift from a tentative "win-lose" stance to one of a "winner's" feeling. Communicating a clear, attractive, and attainable sense of purpose in technical services is a "must" ingredient in motivating and inspiring staff. Leaders, more than managers, function on the emotional and spiritual resources of the organization, collective values and aspirations are very important aspects to followers. Managers, by contrast, deal with physical resources (e.g., new materials, technology) of the organization.

CONCLUSION

Leaders, not managers, will move technical services into the twenty-first century. Followers of these technical services' leaders want to be shown the way and provided the experiences that convince them that their loyalty to the group is a good thing. Leadership is not a matter of hypnosis or blandishment, nor is it a process of exploiting others for extraneous ends. It is a matter of drawing out from individuals those impulses, motives, and efforts that represent them most truly. Leadership in technical services builds confidence and empowers the staff. It is a matter of directing technical services staff, in associated effort, toward personal improvement, integrated desires, and heightened sensibility. Leadership is known by the personalities it enriches. The proof of leading is in the qualitative growth of those being led in technical services, as individuals and as a group.

NOTES

1. Maurice F. Tauber, *Technical Services in Libraries* (New York: Columbia University Press, 1954), p. 4.

2. Warren Bennis and Burt Nanus, *Leaders: The Strategies for Taking Charge* (New York: Harper & Row, 1985), p. 21.

3. James MacGregor Burns, *Leadership* (New York: Harper & Row, 1978), p. 18.

4. Warren Bennis, *The Leaning Ivory Tower* (San Francisco: Jossey-Bass Publishers, 1973), pp. 83-84.

5. Tom Peters and Nancy Austin, *A Passion for Excellence: The Leadership Difference* (New York: Random House, 1985), p. 9.

6. Russell L. Ackoff, *A Concept of Corporate Planning* (New York: John Wiley & Sons, 1970), p. 2.

7. Peter Davis, "Libraries at the Turning Point: Issues in Proactive Planning," *Journal of Library Administration* 1 (Summer 1980): 11-24.

8. Bennis and Nanus, pp. 66-67.

Interaction of Public
and Technical Services:
Collection Development
as Common Ground

Karin E. Ford

As a professional group, librarians are both victims and perpetuators of stereotypes. We are acutely conscious of the stereotype of the fussy, stern, unyielding spinster librarian who demands absolute quiet. Thankfully, that image is quickly being dispelled. However, we have blithely perpetuated another stereotype, often in the guise of managerial efficiency. We are convinced that librarians divide neatly into two personality types: the outgoing, creative, innovative, somewhat disorganized public services (i.e., reference librarian) and the rule-bound, meticulous, timid, well-organized technical services librarian (i.e., cataloger). In the best interests of efficiency and for the good of the unsuspecting public, we have decided to segregate these two types into separate departments where they can put their inherent talents and personality traits to best use.

Of course, these generalizations cannot be made about the personalities of all librarians or the boundaries existing between public and technical services in all libraries. We can easily identify technical services librarians with superb people skills, as well as ones who could never cope with a barrage of reference questions. And some public services librarians are known to be more comfortable with statistics than with the public they supposedly serve, while others can enthusiastically respond to every question, even if they have answered it ten times already that day. Organizationally, for every

Karin E. Ford is Acting Associate Director for Information Services with the Idaho State Library.

41

library that draws sharp boundaries (sometimes chasms) between public and technical services, another library can be found where the boundaries blur or even disappear.

The issues of whether the two departments can, or should, be totally integrated and of whether the "compleat" librarian really exists are discussed elsewhere in this issue. It is the purpose of this article to discuss how interaction can occur to the benefit of the organization, the librarians, and the community being served. A common meeting ground can be found in the activities associated with collection development which may include: title selection, community research, collection assessment and analysis, policy making, and preservation.

This article will discuss how the involvement and interaction of librarians from all departments in collection development activities is: (1) a logical occurrence in light of the changes occurring with increasing automation and emphasis on collection development; (2) an efficient use of the education and talents of all staff; (3) possible when the duties of selectors and the information they require are considered; and (4) being successfully practiced in libraries. Much of the literature cited and many of the examples presented discuss the situations in academic libraries where the organization of collection development activities tends to be more formalized. The interaction of public and technical services librarians for collection development could just as well occur in public and special libraries.

IMPACT OF AUTOMATION

Currently, the primary force motivating change in libraries is the automation of library activities. Automation has precipitated both gradual and dramatic changes in the functions, duties, organizational structure, and staffing patterns of public and technical services. The impact of automation is being felt by libraries and library staffs of all sizes and types. The acquisition of a microcomputer can be as revolutionary for a one-person library as the installation of an integrated automated system can be for a major university library.

Amid the mass of books and articles on automation in libraries — mostly concerning application and implementation — are some thoughtful pieces on the impact of automation on the people who work in libraries and how that work is organized. Sue Ann Harrington notes the "dramatic changes" occurring in libraries with the advent of shared cataloging networks, automated circulation and acquisition systems, online public access catalogs, and online database searching.[1] She concludes that

> as we consider the vast changes that electronic technology is bringing about, it is clear that libraries of the future will be different from those of today. It is also apparent that the library profession must grow and change with the technology.[2]

Harrington sees the most change occurring in technical services. Once technical services units consisted of "workers clustered in small groups around paper files," which required labor-intensive maintenance. Now, files in a shared computer database can contain the information needed for cataloging, acquisition, collection development and, to a lesser extent, serials management. With the computer's assistance, hours spent manually maintaining paper files are reduced to minutes for inputting and accessing data. Much of the cataloging and records maintenance formerly done by professional librarians will increasingly be done by paraprofessional and clerical staff.[3]

Automation's effect on public services activities has been no less dramatic. Online catalogs—inhouse, local, regional, and national—are providing reference staff and their clients with rapid access to bibliographic and holdings information for collections far beyond the walls of a single library. Public access catalogs are dispelling the mysteries of the catalog for library users. When terminals are placed offsite, users can access the collection without entering the building or encountering a librarian. Online databases of periodical citations and full-text are multiplying the information options at a dizzying rate.

Brian Nielsen sees the advent of online database searching as requiring more specialization of public services librarians and changing the division of labor in libraries. In his view, support staff will answer more of the traditional reference questions while librarians conduct searches in the online databases. Rebecca Kroll describes a continuum of reference service, ranging from "the traditional one-on-one reference librarian/patron exploration of printed sources" through the use of online databases instead of print sources for citations and then for quick facts, to end-user searching in the library and offsite.[5] She sees the reference librarian's role changing while progressing along the continuum, moving "away from the reference librarian the source of all knowledge . . . towards the reference librarian as facilitator and educator, helping patrons learn how to help themselves."[6]

That automation is, and will continue, having an impact on the work of technical and public services departments is a point of agreement by most writers on the subject. How that impact will translate into organizational change is a matter of debate. Gregor A. Preston believes that

> at least in the near term, [technical services] staff will simply decrease as a consequence of higher productivity and less original cataloging which result from automation and networks. It is, after all, much simpler to merely reduce staff than it is to revolutionize long-entrenched library divisions and job responsibilities.[7]

Maurice J. Freedman, while warning that "automation is not a panacea, it is a tool," concludes that "differences between departments will be based on professional responsibilities and not strictly on the custody of and control over access to physical files."[8] Michael Gorman states that "it is a mistake to achieve a technological advance and then to try to run the library as usual with the only difference being a slightly improved process."[9]

The theory that automation is encouraging a change in traditional organizational patterns is supported by the experiences of libraries. In 1984, the Association of Research Libraries, Office of Management Studies, Systems and Procedures Exchange Center conducted a survey of ARL member libraries to examine how the organization of public and technical services has changed and what role automation has played in that change. Of the 82 respondents, 46 had a traditional structure and 36 reported some integration of public and technical services. The introduction of "integrated systems" was ranked first in the factors affecting reorganization (although non-automation-related factors were also involved). Materials selection ranked first in both the list of public services functions shared (28 libraries).[10]

MODERN COLLECTION DEVELOPMENT

Before exploring why selection (or collection development) appears to be a logical activity for public and technical services librarians to share, some discussion is needed of how the movement towards more systematic collection development is impacting libraries.

The library profession in the past thirty or forty years has seen an evolution from "book selection" to "collection development" as a professional activity. In describing that evolution, Marcia Pankake defines selection as the examination of the merits of individual titles and the decision to include them in the library's collection. The practice of collection development, on the other hand, requires consideration of the collection as a whole, and includes decisions to add, remove, replace, and preserve in the context of the goals and users of a particular library.[11]

> The preference today for collection development instead of book selection reinforces an emphasis on the quantity of works comprising the collection rather than on individual books. Those who make decisions about materials in the library today not only must be conversant with particular books or other works currently published or in the collection . . . , but they also must have a sense of the whole. How much of the current literature is held? How does the collection compare and relate to other collections on the subject? Is the collection good, and good for what purposes?[12]

Economic factors have probably contributed most to shifting the emphasis from the selection of individual "best" titles to the growth and development of the whole collection. Most libraries in recent years have experienced reduced budgets, or have at least lost purchasing power due to inflation. Any budget increases are usually only forthcoming when the library can justify its existence and convince its governing authority that the library's collection and services are of direct, proven benefit to the community. Use of available fiscal resources is also closely examined and the emphasis is on making the funds stretch farther. At the same time, librarians are faced with a proliferation of information in an ever widening variety of formats.

As a result of these conditions, librarians have exercised their creativity and managerial skills to develop leaner, but more vital collections. Collection development policies are being written and refined to focus selection on those areas of most use to a library's particular community. Resource sharing and cooperative collection development agreements are entered into to supplement the information resources available locally. Sophisticated analytical methods, such as the Research Libraries Group *Conspectus* approach for assessing collection strengths and weaknesses, are being developed and applied in libraries of all types and sizes.

Marcia Pankake summarizes the reorientation in collection development in this way:

> Major concerns in collection development today are neither title-oriented (bibliographic) nor explicitly value-oriented factors, although both still exist. . . . The values important today are technological, scientific, systematic, and the characteristics sought are integration, coordination, and cost efficiency.[13]

We have then the impetus for major changes in the staffing patterns and organizational structures of libraries as a result of automation; coincidental with the need for increased staff time and expertise devoted to planned, systematic collection development.

COLLECTION DEVELOPMENT
AND THE ORGANIZATIONAL STRUCTURE

No doubt, many librarians would argue that there is no need to change staffing patterns, at least where collection development is concerned. There are some libraries where the collection development responsibilities lie in the technical services department, often as an outgrowth of acquisition and conservation activities. In a 1983 article, Larry Earl Bone noted the increasing leadership role that technical services librarians were taking in collection development activities and promotion, especially within ALA. He chided public services librarians for "abdicating [their] responsibility for an important activity."[14] Identifying "quality and user need" as the "two underlying principles of book selection and collection development," Bone states his firm belief that public services librarians have the direct user contact (and the temperament) to evaluate the collection's strengths and weaknesses and its ability to satisfy user needs.[15]

Elizabeth Futas also places collection development squarely in the laps of public services librarians, stating:

It is peculiarly apt for this role to fall upon those in the public services area since, by tradition, they have the closest ties to individual users of the collection, to the selection of materials for the collection, and for the services based upon reference and research collections. From these ties it becomes possible for public services personnel to obtain knowledge of the trends, goals and objectives of users.[16]

A contrasting examination of the role of technical services librarians in evaluation of the collection can be found in an article by Sheila S. Intner. Intner maintains that the qualitative decisions in collection evaluation cannot properly be made without the wealth of quantitative information available from technical services: acquisition statistics and patterns, shelflist analysis, circulation statistics, data on loss rates and patterns, and analysis of interlibrary loan requests. Technical services decisions on the format and maintenance of the catalog and shelflist and preservation decision also impact the work of collection evaluators.[17]

Although warning that quantitative data cannot be the sole basis for collection development decisions, Intner concludes that "to be effective, collection evaluation should be seen as the multidepartmental function it truly is, retaining its links to both public and technical services activities and people. Though collection evaluation is an evaluation, it will prove to be only as good as the information upon which it is based."[18]

Intner makes a strong case for departmental interaction in collection evaluation, but the role she identifies for technical services librarians is that of data gatherer, implying that those making the actual decisions on collection content will be the public services librarians. She states: "Technical services, while contributing importantly to collection growth and change cannot direct them."[19] Interaction between public and technical services is encouraged but the traditional roles and responsibilities are maintained.

SHARING INFORMATION AND EXPERTISE

The assumption is still there that only those librarians with direct, regular contact with library users can know what those users need in a library collection and, therefore, make the correct development decisions. To refute that assumption, an examination is needed of the information and expertise required to make good collection development decisions. If the information and experience gathered by staffing the reference desk is only one part of what is needed, then public services librarians can also be gatherers of data to be shared with and used by collection developers from all parts of the library.

What information do collection developers require? High on the list is a written collection development policy that outlines to both staff and library users the parameters of the particular collection: the subject areas that are (or will be) represented, the depth to which the subjects are covered, and how the collection relates to the needs of the library's community.

Before the development plan described in a collection policy can be carried out, a thorough knowledge of the current state of the collection is necessary. What are the age, physical condition, and quantity of the titles in the subject under scrutiny? How do the titles and authors represented compare with standard bibliographies on the subject? Techniques to assess collection strengths and weaknesses include shelf scanning, shelflist analysis, and title checking against standard lists. Data gathered can be qualified into collection ratings using the Research Libraries Group (RLG) *Conspectus* or a similar tool.[20]

Data on the character and the information needs of the library's community, the extent to which the collection is being used, and how well (or poorly) the collection is meeting the community's needs are also essential. These data can be gathered in a variety of ways, such as formal and informal surveys of users and analysis (by subject) of the patterns of circulation and interlibrary loan. This is the area of collection evaluation where regular, direct contact with users provides opportunities to gather valuable data. However, as Marcia Pankake points out, "these opportunities provide only partial information. Both formal and informal teaching and reference transactions are highly structured encounters with a small portion of the public. The knowledge gained from them about the needs for library materials is necessarily limited."[21] It is very subjective information, based on the librarian's *perceptions* of the users' needs, and of only those users who seek assistance from a librarian. Also, Pankake notes, it does not provide any data on the needs of those who do not use the library at all.[22]

Other data needed for collection development include information on the acquisition process such as status of current orders, ability to obtain foreign language materials or specialized documents and, most importantly, the amount of funds available for purchases.

Collection developers also gather information from reviews, bibliographies, citation studies, and recommendations from users.

Public and technical services librarians do possess different perspectives on the collection, its use, and access to it, which give them each strengths in collection development activities. Librarians in public services have the familiarity with the contents of the collection that comes with regular use, although their knowledge of the reference collection is likely to be more extensive than their knowledge of the circulating collection. They also have daily contact with researchers and users of the collection, an advantage (with limits) in evaluating whether or not the collection meets user needs. If they are subject specialists in a larger library, they should have a good knowledge of the major authors and stay current on contemporary issues and publications in the field.

Librarians working in technical services may possess a familiarity with the collection that comes from regularly reviewing or cataloging the materials that are added to it. They may also handle materials withdrawn from the collection. Their knowledge of the collection's contents may even be more interdisciplinary than that of public services librarians. Catalogers, especially those working with a bibliographic utility, may develop a sense of the unique aspects of the library's collection as they observe what requires original cataloging because another library has not added it to the database. When it comes to a formal assessment of the collection's strengths and weaknesses, technical services librarians may have the advantage, based upon their experience with database manipulation and their thorough knowledge of subject analysis and the classification system.

As librarians, both share a common professional education background. The subject expertise and/or language proficiency that is necessary for developing in-depth collections is usually based upon undergraduate or graduate education outside of library school, or upon personal interest, and may be possessed by technical services librarians as well as by those in public services.

ORGANIZING FOR INTERACTION

It is not enough to simply recognize that both technical and public services librarians possess the education and expertise to participate in collection development activities. Adjustments must be made in the library's organizational structure to permit librarians from different departments to interact and to accomplish collection development work outside of their normal areas. A recent University of Miami outline of "Bibliographer's Duties and Responsibilities" listed the following:

- Public relations;
- Monitoring and information gathering (about the university, and its departments [for the community], the collection, and publishing);
- Management of the existing collection (weeding, replacing, preserving);
- Budgeting and allocation; and
- Continuing education (of the librarian).[23]

None of these duties is beyond the capabilities of either public or technical services librarians. However, to successfully accomplish their responsibilities they need the time and administrative support to analyze and evaluate the existing collection, make contacts with users, select new and replacement material, and continue to learn about their assigned subject area(s) and collection development in general.

Libraries vary greatly in their abilities to adjust their organizational structures to accommodate joint participation and interaction by technical and public services in collection development. Administrators and staff with traditional attitudes toward library operation and staff specializations will be less inclined to break down the barriers between the two areas. Managers and librarians experiencing the changes wrought by automation, and those aware of the need to more efficiently manage information and human resources, will be more receptive to innovation.

There are indications that libraries are beginning to innovate and encourage interaction. Although generalizations to all types and sizes of libraries cannot be made based upon the members of the Association of Research Libraries, two recent studies by ARL's Office of Management Studies, Systems and Procedures Exchange Center (SPEC) illustrate some interesting trends.

A 1984 survey of the ARL members on automation and reorganization of technical and public services [24] found that while none of the 82 respondents reported full integration of public and technical services, 44% reported some "blurring of lines." The duties shared by personnel from different units varied, but "collection development/selection activity is named most often as a shared function."

The survey also found "some evidence of actual new organizational structures . . . in the increased use of committees and task forces to address mutual public/technical services concerns, and multiple reporting relationships (e.g. for collection development, cataloging, and reference activities)."[25]

A report by John R. Kaiser of Pennsylvania State University, published with the above survey, comments on Penn State's appointment and training of "selection-liaison librarians." Criteria for an appointment include:

(1) formal training and education in a given subject area; (2) . . . interest in and the capability of developing subject expertise through the process of self-education; (3) . . . the potential for growth in the area of collection management and development; [and] (4) . . . the approval of the librarian's department head [to] . . . participate in collection activities.

Kaiser notes that

no where do we restrict a librarian from applying for a Selection-Liaison appointment because of the area in which she or he works. Thus we have people in these positions from Acquisitions, Cataloging, Lending Services, General Reference, Documents, Periodicals and Microforms."[26]

A SPEC survey, *Collection Development Organization and Staffing*, found that:

The organization of collection development and management functions usually falls into one of three patterns: (1) a staff largely composed of full-time bibliographers with responsibilities assigned by academic department, language or subject area; (2) a decentralized staff, where a significant number of professional staff have some collection development responsibilities; and (3) a staff with some combination of full-time bibliographers and other full-time staff who work as selectors part-time.[27]

Part-time selectors were used to some extent by 50 of the 53 responding libraries, a situation which encourages the involvement of staff from various departments. The study noted that over the past three years . . . there has been a movement toward using part-time selectors from other departments, including the non-public services areas of acquisitions and cataloging. Among the 53 responding libraries, the approximate percentage of total professional staff involved in collection development ranged from 10 percent to 75 percent, with an average of 40 percent.[28]

CONCLUSION

Managing the interaction of staff from different departments for common collection development activities may be a difficult organizational adjustment for many libraries but it is not impossible. To operate successfully, it requires coordination by a manager with the authority to cross departmental boundaries. In smaller libraries, that coordinator may be the director. In larger ones, the trend is towards appointment of a collection development librarian who reports to the director or the assistant director.

Communication among staff involved in collection development is essential. Staff must be thoroughly familiar with the collection development policy and involved in making any changes to it. They must frequently share information—formally and informally—on the collection, its users, and the materials they have or are planning to acquire.

Collection development can be a common ground for the meeting of public and technical services librarians. Their combined expertise can be a powerful, positive force in shaping a well-developed, responsive collection. When given the opportunity to interact, they will prove that the traditional structural barriers are superfluous and will lay another stereotype to rest.

NOTES

1. Sue Anne Harrington, "The Changing Environment in Technical Services," *Technical Services Quarterly* 4 (Winter 1986):8.

2. Harrington, p. 10.

3. Harrington, pp. 10-16.

4. Brian Nielsen, Online Reference and the 'Great Change,' in *Online Catalogs, Online Reference: Converging Trends. Proceedings of a Library and Information Technology Association Preconference Institute, June 23-24, 1983, Los Angeles*, ed. Brian Aveney and Brett Butler (Chicago: American Library Association, 1984), p. 77.

5. Rebecca Kroll, "The Ripple Effect: The Impact of Online on Library Op-

erations," in *Dollars and Sense: Implications of the New Online Technology for Managing the Library. Proceedings of a Conference Program Held in New York City, June 29, 1986*, ed. Bernard F. Pasqualini (Chicago: American Library Association, 1987), p. 40.

6. Kroll, p. 44.

7. Gregor A. Preston, "How Will Automation Affect Cataloging Staff?" *Technical Services Quarterly* 1 (Fall/Winter 1983):131.

8. Maurice J. Freedman, "Automation and the Future of Technical Services," *Library Journal* 109 (June 15, 1984):1203.

9. Michael Gorman, "The Future of Serials Control and Its Administrative Implications for Libraries," in *Serials Automation for Acquisition and Inventory Control*, ed. William Gray Potter and Arlene Farber Sirkim (Chicago: American Library Association, 1981), p. 126.

10. *Automation and Reorganization of Technical and Public Services*, Association of Research Libraries, Office of Management Studies, Systems and Procedures Exchange Center Kit 112 (Washington, DC, March 1985), p. 4.

11. Marcia Pankake, "From Book Selection to Collection Management: Continuity and Advance in an Unending Work," in *Advances in Librarianship* vol. 13, ed. Wesley Simonton (Orlando, FL: Academic Press, 1984), pp. 199-201.

12. Pankake, p. 201.

13. Pankake, p. 206.

14. Larry Earl Bone, "Noblesse Oblige: Collection Development as a Public Service Responsibility," *The Reference Librarian* 9 (Fall/Winter 1983):65.

15. Bone, pp. 68-70.

16. Elizabeth Futas, "The Role of Public Services in Collection Evaluation," *Library Trends* 33 (Winter 1985):397.

17. Sheila S. Intner, "Responsibilities of Technical Service Librarians to the Process of Collection Evaluation," *Library Trends* 33 (Winter 1985):417-33.

18. Intner, p. 434.

19. Intner, p. 434.

20. For an overview of evaluation techniques, see: Paul H. Mosher, "Quality and Library Collections: New Directions in Research and Practice in Collection Evaluation," in *Advances in Librarianship* vol. 13, ed. Wesley Simonton (Orlando, FL: Academic Press, 1984), pp. 211-38.

21. Pankake, p. 191.

22. Pankake, p. 191.

23. University of Miami, "Bibliographer's Duties and Responsibilities: An Outline," in *Collection Development Organization and Staffing in ARL Libraries*, Association of Research Libraries, Office of Management Studies, Systems and Procedures Exchange Center Kit 131 (Washington, DC, February 1987), pp. 52-55.

24. *Automation and Reorganization*, SPEC Kit 112.

25. B.J. Busch, "Automation and Reorganization of Technical and Public Services," *SPEC Flyer* #112 (March 1985):1-2.

26. John R. Kaiser, "The Selection-Liaison Project at Penn State," in *Automation and Reorganization of Technical and Public Services* SPEC Kit 112 (Washington, DC, March 1985), pp. 78-79.

27. James E. Bobick, "Collection Development Organization and Staffing," *SPEC Flyer* #131 (February 1987):1.

28. Bobick, pp. 1-2.

Changing Staffing Patterns in Technical Services Since the 1970s: A Study in Change

Virginia Lee Andrews
Carol Marie Kelley

Library assistants have faced increasing responsibilities in all types of libraries for many years. At Texas Tech the classification "library assistant" refers to personnel who execute tasks that fall between the duties of professional staff and clerical or student personnel. There is no consistent name for this group of library employees in library literature; for this article they are called library assistants in particular or support staff in general. The purpose of this article is to share the changes that have evolved in library assistant workflow at the Texas Tech University Libraries since 1974. The causes for these changes and the reactions of both professional and support staff are discussed. Specific workflow patterns and training plans are also discussed.

HISTORICAL BACKGROUND

In 1970/71 before the introduction of OCLC to the Texas Tech University Library, there were four processing units, all operating separately: the Catalog Department, the Order Department, the Periodicals Department, and Government Documents. Support staff in these areas were classified as clerks, clerk-typists I-II, and library assistants I-II.

The Catalog Department had nine professional catalogers, five

Virginia Lee Andrews is Automation Coordinator, and Carol Marie Kelley is Head of Acquisitions at Texas Tech University Libraries, Lubbock, TX.

clerk-typists, a library assistant I, a library assistant II, and student assistants. The professional staff was responsible for copy and original cataloging and revision of the continuous filing processes in the public card catalog and the nonpublic shelflist. The support staff was responsible for the physical processing of materials, adding and changing holdings statements to the shelflist and public catalog, and the production of catalog card sets via a Multilith offset press. The students provided assistance to both the professional and support staff in all areas. The largest concentration of student staff was in card filing. Students processed both the card sets produced by the catalog unit and those purchased from vendors.

The Order Department had two professional librarians, one library assistant, six clerk typists I-II, and student assistants. The department was divided into selection, ordering, and receiving. The professional staff was responsible for book selection and vendor assignment. The support staff was responsible for verification, sending orders, and processing shipments. These responsibilities included approval plans, firm orders, and standing orders. In addition an accounting clerk processed payments from all areas of the library and worked with the director and the associate directors, in addition to the Order Department.

The Periodicals Department had two professional librarians, two clerk-typists, two library assistants I-II, and student assistants. The professional staff selected periodical titles, supervised the upkeep of periodical records and the public service desk, and were members of the science reference staff. The support staff was responsible for periodical ordering and renewal, check-in, and binding. The student assistants shelved materials and helped the support staff in their responsibilities.

Government Documents had two professional librarians, one clerk, one clerk-typist, and student assistants. The professional staff helped patrons use the collection, continuously pulled important documents from the shelves and kept them on shelves adjacent to their desks, supervised the receipt and check-in of depository shipments, collected and stored superseded volumes that were cataloged and shelved in the general collection, and operated the department as a separate functional entity. The full time support staff was responsible for check-in of materials and assistance at the documents reference desk when needed. The students shelved and helped in processing tasks.

INTRODUCTION TO AUTOMATION

In September 1974, the Texas Tech Library joined OCLC. Two OCLC 100 terminals were installed in the Catalog Department for searching, inputting original cataloging, and editing for card sets. OCLC training was provided by what is now the AMIGOS Network, based in Dallas. The training stressed that the system was for support staff and that use of OCLC would free catalog librarians of repetitive tasks. Automation allowed time for the professional catalogers to concentrate on specific formats, subject assignments, authority control, or other areas requiring their expertise.

After the initial training, the catalog managers began investigating the use of OCLC in the current workflow. Although some of the staff was resistant to OCLC, the decision to alter workflow to fully utilize it became inevitable. Most of the professional staff did not like the quality of records in the system and were skeptical of accepting other members' cataloging. The support staff feared automation and subsequently questioned their job security. There was also some reluctance from the support staff toward added responsibilities as the workflow changed.

The senior catalog librarian was given the approval of the department chair to begin reorganizing workflow. Most of the staff received an OCLC manual to study the procedures for applying OCLC to the workflow. The support staff received the same treatment and exposure to OCLC as did the professional staff. It was believed the training the support staff possessed in basic filing, authority control, cataloging, and card production could be used as a basis for training for online searching and editing for card production.

Several factors resulting from use of OCLC aided in raising morale and increasing the confidence of the staff:

— the backlog decreased
— efficiency increased,
— tasks were more interesting,
— the staff felt important.

The first major change in personnel resulting from the reorganization of workflow was the creation of a position to take the responsibility for training the staff on OCLC. The position was to be held by a library assistant, rather than a librarian. The library assistant who was obviously the outstanding terminal operator was reclassified at a higher level and was given responsibility for training all new OCLC terminal operators. This promotion, plus the involvement of the support staff in departmental planning, added to the increased morale mentioned above. Generally it required more work to train the professional staff to accept the increased responsibility of the library assistants and the changes in professional workflow than it did for the library assistants to accept the changes in their workflow.

The changes in workflow permitted library assistants to edit and produce card sets, input original cataloging from tag sheets, and input LC copy. Professional staff were producing tag sheets for original cataloging and online revision. They also used the OCLC system for verification of names and research.

CONVERSION OF MONOGRAPHS

Within a year it was possible to begin a major retrospective conversion project using existing staff. The support staff read the shelflist and searched OCLC for matching records for monographic titles. Records that matched the shelflist cards were identified, edited and updated or produced, if the card set in the catalog was outdated or in poor condition. As with current workflow, problems were routed to the professional staff. Titles not yet in the OCLC database were skipped.

The retroconversion of monographs (due to the existing pricing for use of OCLC during prime time) was being done in limited time blocs. In 1984, the installation of an M300 workstation and the Cataloging Microenhancer software improved the workflow considerably. The workstation so improved the workflow that more were ordered to replace the older series of terminals. Some increased activity in the retro project followed. Items were searched and OCLC numbers recorded for nonprime time downloading, edited offline, and uploaded the following evening. When the new version of the microenhancer with the save file function became available, the retrospective project started in full swing again. With the regular workflow having improved so much with the new software, more terminals and time were released to the retro project. Student assistants, under the joint supervision of a cataloger and a library assistant, were scheduled at the terminals on a regular basis for the purpose of downloading with the save file function; the completion of retro began to escalate. This increased productivity also caused a backlog of older items for our professional staff to upgrade to AACR2 cataloging for original input. Since the amount of professional staff was limited, it became necessary to adjust the workflow, especially with a push to complete as much as possible for the future online catalog. Anticipating an online catalog within the next three to four years and not wanting to slow down the project, the decision to increase the original cataloging staff during a mandatory hiring freeze presented a problem.

During planning sessions, two library assistants volunteered to be trained to alleviate the situation. Intensive training classes with AACR2 rules, LC rule interpretations, and the OCLC bibliographic input standards were conducted by the OCLC Coordinator. Since the "Retro" books had call numbers and subject headings, the library assistants and the Serials Cataloger were soon filling out tag or input sheets for these books. The challenge of cataloging the older material utilizing the name authority and subject heading verification as well as the rules for descriptive cataloging raised the morale of the support staff. As the ones designated to do the original cataloging fell behind in their other duties, other library assistants and the student assistants stepped in to pick up the slack.

This cooperative effort within the Catalog Department has been the prevailing attitude in the Texas Tech Library in other areas and between departments. The retrospective conversion for the monographic collection, which is in its third and inputting phase, is still in process at this writing. At its completion, all nonmicroform monographic titles will be on tape or in an online system.

CONVERSION OF SERIALS

With the success experienced in the Catalog Department, the next step in implementing automated processing into workflow was to use the OCLC Serials Control Subsystem to transfer serial holdings data from manual files beginning in the mid-1970s. The Periodicals Department had been a separate unit. The check-in and payment files for periodicals were moved to the area adjoining the Catalog Department and combined with the existing Order Department to create the Acquisitions Department. One professional and one library assistant from the Periodicals Department joined the Acquisitions Department staff. The work of the department was then divided into traditional monograph and serial units.

Another library assistant and the binding files from the Periodicals Department were moved to a newly created Bindery Department which assumed responsibility for all physical processing of both new and old materials.

When the OCLC Serials Control Subsystem was released, the serials section staff began training in both the serial bibliographic and local data records procedures on the newly released OCLC Serials Control Subsystem. No one at OCLC, the Networks, or the member libraries knew exactly how to apply the system's capabilities to the serials workflow within libraries. The successful experience with reorganization of workflow within the Catalog Department provided support for applying similar techniques in serials processing.

The standing order file was the first file converted to machine readable form. The number of terminals in the technical processing area increased to four. Once again support staff participated in planning. The major difference with serials was that two subsystems were being accessed: the cataloging subsystem and the new serials control subsystem. The OCLC Coordinator, the serials cataloger, the serials acquisitions librarian, and a library assistant in the newly created combined acquisitions/serials department were trained first; they planned the project workflow. This group began training others to work on the serial project. The terminal operators with the most experience edited bibliographic records; those with less training created the local data records. Within a few months, training expanded to include the entire technical processing staff. All staff from heads of the processing departments to student assistants were scheduled for time slots four nights a week and Saturday mornings. At first morale dropped a little as staff did not look forward to spending an evening in the library; however, after the project was underway, the majority enjoyed having a morning or afternoon off during the week.

By the end of the standing order project, several standards for effective workflow that could be applied to all future serial conversion projects had been created:

- Check-in files were never duplicated. Once an online check-in record was "built," serial receipts went to the OCLC terminal alone for check-in.
- Both support staff and professional staff planned projects together. The support staff were allowed to take on major responsibilities and were reclassified if appropriate.

— "Flex time" allowed projects to continue in the evening when terminal response time was faster and there were fewer interruptions.
— The staff was trained to work at the terminal, rather than on paper. During these projects, terminal operators had current checkin files and the shelflist cards at their workstations. They searched for a matching bibliographic record, edited it, updated the file or ordered cards (if title changes were involved or our cards were outdated), and built the serial holdings record.
— Problem titles went to professional staff to avoid delaying the terminal operators in the regular workflow. The professional staff solved the problem and returned the cards and tag sheets to the terminal supervisor.
— Intensive classes and training sessions were held two or three times a year to maintain staff awareness and to update staff concerning both bibliographic and local data record tags and their applications.

The standing order project was followed by the much larger and more complex Kardex project which involved conversion of 16 cabinets of records to machine readable form. Since the periodical check-in process had to continue and staff did not want to duplicate check-in records, the night crews became critical to the success of the project. The entire Technical Processing staff participated in the first read through of the Kardex. The serials staff planned to work on their regular duties during the day, as did staff in other processing departments. However, after about a third of the Kardex titles were online, the serials personnel found themselves performing both the current check-in, the claiming process and the conversion project during regular work time. Tough problems could be resolved during the day. The student assistants who were responsible for check-in liked working at night; therefore, some current check-in was done in the evenings.

The second reading of the Kardex was done by the Serial Acquisitions and Serials Cataloging staffs, allowing the Cataloging and Bindery Department staffs to resume their own projects. At this writing the Kardex project has been completed and the personnel in Serials Cataloging and Serial Acquisitions have turned their attention to processing those serial titles in the shelflist that were not included in the Kardex or Standing Order files.

In 1983 a LSCA grant was received to create the West Texas Union List using OCLC. A temporary full time library assistant III position to supervise student assistants, as well as the student assistant time was funded by the grant. The grant staff worked in the evenings using six OCLC terminals. Since holdings statements were already online, students converted the existing holdings statements to summary statement fields, creating the union list records.

CONVERSION OF GOVERNMENT DOCUMENTS

Buoyed by the success of the Cataloging and Serials Projects and the changes in the workflow of those units led to a review of the processing procedures within the Documents Department. The Documents Department, although not in technical processing, has its own "technical services unit." In 1979 an OCLC terminal was placed in the Documents Processing area. There are three professionals and three and one half time library assistants on the Documents staff providing both public and technical services.

A study of documents receipts revealed that the department's shipments averaged at least sixty-five percent serials, including monographic series. Beginning in January 1980, all incoming material was cataloged on OCLC and check-in records were built for serials. As in the Cataloging and Acquisitions Departments, support staff was given increased responsibility and later received higher classifications. Within a year of beginning check-in, Documents installed a second terminal. During the next two years, a monographic retrospective conversion project ran concurrently with the serials retrospective conversion project. At this writing the serial conversion project is still in process while the monographic conversion project has been put on hold due to lack of adequate personnel.

IMPACT ON LIBRARY ASSISTANTS

There are several consistent changes that have occurred in each of the Texas Tech Library departments involved with automation:

— As indicated earlier, support staff was given increased responsibility. The number of tasks assigned to support staff increased. In all cases a central training position was created.
— The clerk I-II, clerk typist I-II and library assistant I classifications were no longer used in the departments that had auto-

mated processing. More supervisory positions classified as library assistant III-IVs were created.
— Automated departments increased the number of library assistants used. This was not the result of the conversion projects, but was the result of OCLC creating a quicker, more efficient workflow.

PLANNING

The Texas Tech Library has never met the ratios of professional vs. clerical staff indicated as desirable in library literature. Likewise the number of professional staff members has been low for a library the size of Texas Tech. The limited manpower resources have forced departments to train and delegate to library assistants tasks that might be assigned to professionals in other libraries. Automation and the belief that it enhances library assistant duties provided the momentum to experiment with newer workflows.

Over the years the technical services staff has worked together to plan the workflow for these projects:

— Retrospective conversion of all records. At Texas Tech this retrospective conversion has always been performed by existing staff rather than contracting to vendors. The impact on library assistant personnel has been discussed in an earlier section of this article.
— Application of AACR2 cataloging changes. Library assistants were included in the education process and later in the application of the rules. Several were superior workers in identifying materials needing recataloging and in performing authority work. One who was outstanding in authority control was reclassified to a supervisory position. Thus the cumbersome task of identifying discrepancies in the manual authority file and the OCLC online file (in addition to reordering card sets for the public catalog) could be removed from professional staff and assigned to library assistant level staff.
— Conversion of collections housed outside the library building, or in the building but not originally included in the cataloged collection has been planned by both support staff and librarians.
— Providing links between automated workflows and manual workflows. This is a continuous problem that will plague us

until we are fully automated. We have discovered that library assistant personnel are able to identify and successfully work through the problems of mixed workflows.

An example of the latter is that the library assistant staff in Acquisitions, Documents, Materials Processing, and Serials Cataloging create and control serial record information with success. However, serial holdings are stored in two automated, incompatible systems which link to another incompatible microcomputer binding system. These must then link with a manual shelflist and additional manual binding files which supplement the microcomputer file. All of this information is controlled by library assistant managers and their subordinates.

ORGANIZATION

The general organization of the technical processing departments followed traditional compartmentalized lines in 1974. The inclusion of the entire processing staff in the first serial retrospective conversion project was the first attempt to cross departmental responsibility. From 1975 until 1982 the Acquisitions Department had the responsibility for the bibliographic and holdings data conversion of serials. In 1983, all cataloging of serials became the responsibility of the Serials Cataloging staff within the Catalog Department. Even with the responsibility returning to traditional lines in 1983, the majority of the processing staffs continued to be scheduled at OCLC terminals in either serial acquisitions or cataloging.

In 1984/85 a new Associate Director of Libraries for Technical Processing formed a task force to study the organization of the entire division. The Task Force consisted of five professional librarians and five library assistants: a cataloger, the Head of Acquisitions, the Head of Materials Processing, the OCLC Coordinator, a bibliographer, two library assistants from Acquisitions, two from Materials Processing and one from Cataloging. These members were elected by their peers.

The objectives of the task force were to recommend physical rearrangement of the areas to provide better access, to assist in ridding the division of feelings of territoriality, and to create a more attractive work environment. Each area carefully examined why tasks were performed and where there was duplicated effort and unnecessary work. Within nine months a floor plan was drawn up and accepted by personnel in the technical processing division.

The result was the beginning of an overall self-examination which is still in process at this writing. At the same time for various reasons including changes in patron needs, retirements and staffing shortages, major organizational changes began throughout the Library which further changed the roles of both librarians and library assistants. The Public Services, Technical Processing, and Administrative Services Divisions were combined into one division; it was named Information Access and Systems. The Associate Director of Libraries for Technical Processing became the Associate Director of Libraries for Information Access and Systems. The OCLC Coordinator became the Automation Coordinator, responsible for CLSI as well as for OCLC, and began planning for further automation. The Head of Documents became the Head of Reference and Documents. Reference began to examine broader use of library assistant personnel. Vacant professional and library assistant positions were reviewed and the professional positions and some support staff positions were made multifunctional, assigned to different departments.

The University's Personnel Department audited all library staff possible creation of new position classifications due to the increased responsibility of library assistants. As a result of this audit, four library assistants received a newly created title: Library Unit Supervisor. These were the support staff supervisors of Circulation, Database Inputting, Database Maintenance, and Documents Processing.

After the Technical Processing Task Force completed its review of all of the processing areas, the Acquisitions Department was interested in a further review of its organization of its workflow since an acquisitions/serials system was to be acquired. In 1986/87 the Head of Acquisitions formed a task force to recommend a reorganization of the department that would better use an automated system that would impact on all phases of the department's activities. Now the Acquisitions Department is no longer divided into serials and monographs units. Instead it is organized into:

— An Order/Verification Unit with a Library Assistant IV as supervisor. This unit verifies and orders all materials, keeps subscription records, and interacts with vendors and publishers. The unit consists of two Library Assistant IIs, students, and the supervisor.

— A Receiving Unit with the Head of Acquisitions as acting supervisor. This unit receives the materials from subscriptions, standing orders, firm orders, and the approval plan. It also routes samples to subject liaisons and maintains the approval review area. The unit consists of two Library Assistant IIIs, a Library Assistant II, students, and the supervisor.

— A Maintenance Unit with a Library Assistant IV as head. This unit builds and controls holdings records on the OCLC Serials Control Subsystem, the OCLC Union List, and the local database used to produce a holdings printout. It interacts with Serials Cataloging and the subject liaisons. The unit consists of two Library Assistant IIs, a Library Assistant III, students, and the supervisor.

The supervisors of the three subunits of Acquisitions are responsible to the Head of Acquisitions who is responsible to the Associate Director of Libraries for Information Access and Systems.

The Cataloging Department was also in need of some additional reorganization to cope with both inevitable personnel changes and the preparation for an online catalog. It was then reorganized into four units with each unit head reporting directly to the Associate Director of Libraries for Information Access and Systems. The four units are:

— Database Inputting with a Library Unit Supervisor as head. This unit is responsible for the day to day card production of all new material; the inputting of original cataloging and LC copy into OCLC; and the continuing retrospective conversion project. The unit consists of two Library Assistant IIs and the supervisor.

— Database Maintenance with a Library Unit Supervisor as head. This unit is responsible for card catalog maintenance, CLSI (circulation system) maintenance, inventory control, name and subject authority control, and adding continuations to the shelflist. The unit consists of two Library Assistant IIIs, a Library Assistant II, students, and the supervisor.

— General Cataloging with a librarian as head. This unit is responsible for all original cataloging except serials. The unit consists of five catalogers and the supervisor. Some of the catalogers also work in other areas of the library.

— Serials Cataloging with the Serials Cataloger as head. This unit is responsible for all of the serial cataloging, copy and original, serials card production, and retrospective conversion of serial bibliographic records. The unit consists of a Library Assistant IV, two Library Assistant IIs, students, and the supervisor.

All of the support staff in each unit are cross-trained and work in other areas as needed. All staff are still involved in brainstorming and planning of workflow and procedures.

CONCLUSION

There are several characteristics of the Texas Tech Library staff and the library's organizational structure that have made experiments with library assistant staff possible:

— Longevity of employees. In September 1986, for example, the Cataloging staff had a record of combined years of service at Texas Tech (professional and support, excluding students) of 201 years for 15.3 FTE employees. This long record of service provides an excellent opportunity to train and expand the expertise of the support staff. The support staff's years of service alone total over 65 years for 8.5 FTE employees.

— Providing education. Support staff are encouraged to take regular classes at the university and to attend relevant workshops and seminars. Continuous developmental opportunities are offered by the Library's Personnel Office. Library Assistants are included in workshops and classes that pertain to their work responsibilities and also are allowed to attend appropriate area workshops.

— Staff Involvement. The inclusion of the support staff in the planning and implementation of projects and procedures and on standing committees increases their knowledge and self-image. Library Assistants are also encouraged to participate in library organizations. One support staff member coauthored a paper with a librarian and presented it at the 1987 Texas Library Association Convention. A library assistant from Texas Tech was also the first recipient of a stipend awarded by the Texas Library Association to attend its state convention.

Through continued self-examination and review of vacant positions, every library assistant position has been reviewed and all job descriptions have been rewritten. With most library areas now reporting to one associate director, the entire library staff is embarking on a new era of cooperation and exchange of personnel. Each department or unit head reporting to this associate director is a member of the Information Access and Systems Council. Ideas and project plans are presented to the group. The departments and/or units then exchange or join with other areas to accomplish the goals or objectives as presented in Council.

As we progress toward total automation at the Texas Tech Library, we hope to create a work environment conducive for handling the most difficult problems. Our philosophy of maximum manpower and talent utilization, cooperative sharing of resources, and open communication has been and will continue to be the vehicle for a successful transition to total automation.

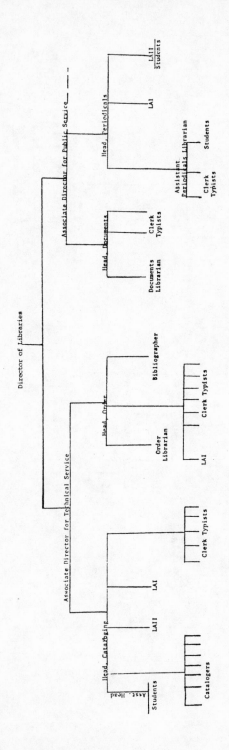

ORGANIZATIONAL CHART FOR
PROCESSING UNITS
FOR 1970/71

Director of Libraries

Associate Director for Technical Service

Associate Director for Public Service

Head, Cataloging

Asst. Head

Students

LAII

LAI

Clerk Typists

Catalogers

Head, Order

Order Librarian

LAI

Clerk Typists

Bibliographer

Head, Documents

Documents Librarian

Clerk Typists

Head, Periodicals

Assistant Periodicals Librarian

Clerk Typists

Students

LAI

LAII

Students

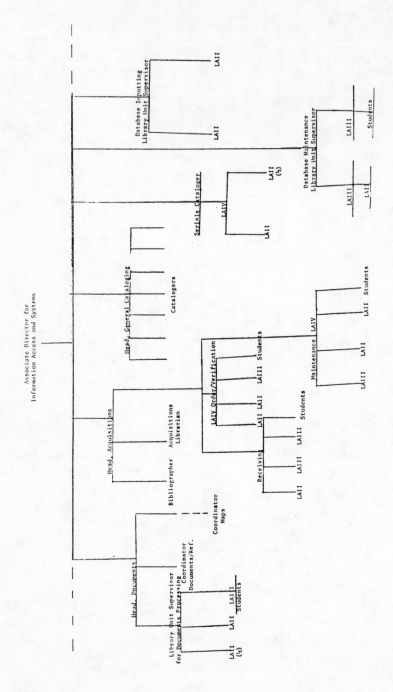

ORGANIZATIONAL CHART FOR
PROCESSING UNITS
FOR 1986/87

70

Staff Considerations
in Technical Services:
The Chameleon Approach

Constance L. Foster

Librarians explore the impact of technological change on their professional surroundings with as many cautions, pithy sayings, and prophecies as Benjamin Franklin and Alexander Pope created in their epigrams about stitches, stones, and fools. This force of change, propelled by the advent of computers in the library, has caused many a librarian to cling to a past condition buried within the pages of the red book or card catalog, to project simple messages and occasional humor on posters, and to search frantically through *Punch* for an appropriate cartoon to make light of a frustrating situation. The thrust into the next decade of library technical services does not lead us to a timely quote from Lancaster, Boss, or Avram; instead we literally go "back to the future" to Heraclitus, who flourished around 500 B.C. Without formal libraries, certainly devoid of dreams of technological wonders, and lacking scholarly journals to nurture his professional development, he perceived that "nothing is permanent but change."[1]

THE STABILITY OF CHANGE

The axiom of change as reality, constancy, and permanency is indeed one which we can tape to our walls or emblazon on a wooden plaque. To accept this and immediately set it aside is essential so that all library personnel can develop, prosper, and truly enjoy productive roles soon. We already lag in uses of computers

Constance L. Foster is Serials Supervisor and Associate Professor, Department of Library Automation and Technical Services, Western Kentucky University, Bowling Green, KY.

for technical resources, internal effectiveness, and patron services. What we readily acknowledge as new and transformational — specifically change by virtue of computer systems within libraries — assumes a less overwhelming dimension when we recall Heraclitus' observation during a much simpler era.

For technical services staff the routine and extraordinary tasks that have been altered by automation require that we become as chameleons and adapt to our surroundings in such a masterful, flexible way that we survive, and in doing so, thrive. Even though the idea of change is ancient, the demands we confront are recent; they dictate constant initiative, planning, action, and evaluation. How to cope with these technological transitions and suggestions for viable work settings as we lock into routines created by automation mean occasionally stepping back, breathing deeply, and becoming like the fly on the wall to assess fairly and realistically our futures.

COMPUTER CONSEQUENCES

Although the twenty-first century does not promise a paperless library, we will enter the year 2000 with veteran experiences supporting the tremendous alterations in technical services operations, accomplishments, and resources. This evolution of a systems-oriented library produces the following effects:

- Requires staff to be flexible, sensitive, and creative.
- Forces some persons to seek jobs elsewhere or take early retirement.
- Defines new skills desired for data entry, information retrieval, and analysis of information, skills involving accuracy and prompting accountability at all levels of staffing.
- Reshapes jobs, requires training, and creates challenges for work away from the computer when the system is down or must be shared.
- Considers the work setting as a critical element in achieving a productive services unit.
- Necessitates financial planning for acquiring, leasing, and maintaining systems as well as for training personnel in the use of these tools.
- Diffuses the traditional distinctions between the public and technical services areas by increasing interdependence for information access and by allowing additional services that previously were not feasible.

These basic considerations directly relate to personnel needs as a result of computerized conditions that did not really exist in libraries twenty years ago. Such computer consequences have created a problem that Craig Brod identifies as "technostress."[2] To carry Brod's concept from the corporate setting into the library does not have to result in clinical sessions with organizational psychologists and psychotherapists as a final effort to treat those who cannot function within an automated setting. We do have to balance the myriad of stresses induced by the computer, yet there are equally therapeutic methods in a nonclinical sense for us, preventive ones rather than curative. Instead of psychotherapy we consider technotherapy to prevent, relieve, or eliminate tensions in our evolution towards highly specialized information referral and retrieval centers. Technotherapy implies recognition of change and flexibility in dealing with it. We cannot fail to understand the role of the computer as a tool and to contend with its presence in a reasonable, thoughtful manner. Such understanding will assure, support, and enrich library technical services staff in the next decades.

REASSESSMENT OF ATTITUDES

Usually a library employee assumes a position with a predefined set of duties, responsibilities, expectations, and qualifications. No sooner does he or she read a procedures manual hastily prepared by a departing employee than certain processes cease to exist and additional ones appear. Welcome the computer, followed by it peripherals and installation logistics! Shoving the manual under a *Cataloging Service Bulletin*, this new person suddenly faces a confused future with a monolithic machine precipitating a flurry of activity. The computer, meanwhile, lies dormant amid all this transition until its coaxial cables, modem, and ports achieve a unity of purpose. Then the new employee, along with all the other staff, begins to adjust to the computer's schedules, codes, software, noise levels, furniture rearrangement, training sessions, and concurrently continues what few stable routines are left. The computer does come first in this context and demands our all. Once everyone adjusts and truly believes that the computer only does what it is told to do, the gargantuan projects spew forth from someone's directives: retrospective conversion, elimination of paper files, budget recodes, management reports, and so on. Welcome stress! That new employee, now discarding the outdated procedures manual, thumbs through training booklets and detailed implementation plans, listens to discussions on how the computer will affect work flow, and attempts to complete manual tasks while learning automated ones.

Unless we can remain aware of many levels of operation at the same time, technology will generate a beat-the-clock mentality. Increased workloads may seem productive at the time, but for bibliographic databases to be useful, accuracy and quality of input have to emerge as goals. As Brod wisely states, "The computer now determines the flow of work through the office, and the staffers set their work rhythm to fit the computer's pace. People expect a faster flow of reports, with fewer visible errors."[3] The fallacy of completing more work sooner and increasing tasks to replace that free time is one that should be avoided at all costs. The more critical issue is to accomplish the same tasks in different and better ways, engage in new services, and eliminate outmoded procedures. We cannot afford to transfer one-on-one a manual process to an automated one. In trying to approach operations with this idea, we shortchange ourselves and greatly miss the benefits of the technology. Computers as tools offer librarians the advantage of faster retrieval of information, almost instantaneous corrections, timely production of reports and innovative procedures. These computer progressions are healthy ones.

Because technical services staff in libraries usually experience the impact of automation first, while the public services staff patiently await the results of all these systems and networks, Shirley Leung feels that "it is more likely for technical services to be asked to explain why one particular item is not cataloged on a timely basis than to be complimented for having a large number of items [processed] expeditiously."[4] For catalog, acquisitions, and serials staff the pressure mounts, accountability increases, and patience wears thin. By involving all units of the library in general planning sessions and informational exchanges, these questions can decrease in direct proportion to the degree of understanding achieved.

STRATEGIES OF A CHAMELEON

Where then are we headed in our therapeutic quest to alleviate "technostress" within libraries? Rosabeth Moss Kanter comments that organizations will change and that the people within them must also for "organizations need innovation to shift from the present tendency to deal with their tasks in a relatively single-minded, top-directed way and to a capacity to respond innovatively, locally and promptly to a whole variety of organizational contingencies — to change shape, so to speak."[5] Remember the chameleon: flexible, sensitive, and successful in adapting to its environment by being alert to changes and anticipating them. We, too, find these qualities essential for our technological survival.

Within technical services these organizational changes mean restructuring and realigning positions, assessing the quality of work life, accounting for financial outlay, and improving channels of communication. As Henriette Avram notes, "Changes in organization make people uncomfortable, change necessitates retraining, technical change brings into the library a whole new breed of technicians that managers must manage, old-timers are not happy, and new-timers are impatient with the old."[6]

Managerial staff particularly need to be alert to signs of resistance to change. We all seek stability in our daily routines, like the telephone placed on the right side of the desk, stapler to the left, coffee breaks at 9:30 a.m. and lunch at noon. Such routines give us time to hold on while all about us, change occurs. Kanter remarks that the irony in change is in allowing "sufficient calendar time to make it work, as well as enough available participant time to engage in planning, communication, and reflection about the appropriateness of job and project activities."[7] Through deliberate communication to as many people as possible, those responsible for implementing change in an area can prepare those most affected by the new surroundings and tools.

THINKING WITH BOTH BRAINS

Supportive of the dilemma we face in the emphasis on different skills and qualifications for technical services positions is the theory of the human brain described by Thomas Blakeslee. He refers to the functions of the two halves of the brain as a partnership. The left half of the brain handles language and logical thinking, while the right half deals with images and spatial concepts. Although each half can atrophy, we need to develop and call upon both halves to balance ourselves.[8] Hence, skills needed to complete tasks successfully shift "from just manual dexterity to the intellectual ability to absorb, organize, and interpret information, as well as greater capacity for concentrated attention and process conceptualization, because of closer inter-relationships with other jobs," according to Grace Bulaong.[9] Basic work requirements transfer from typing sixty words per minute to the ability to input data via computer terminal coupled with the ability to interpret information and explain processes. Although we may value someone who is lock-step logical in approaching and reacting to every situation, future productive work traits lean towards hiring people who possess creativity, analytical and verbal acuity. In other words, those who have developed both halves of their brains. Technology may remove much of the intuitive process that we once knew, yet that same technological influence impels us to hone our verbal and critical skills if we are to offer effective services within a highly competitive information industry.

RESHAPING JOBS

While maintaining an orientation to the total library organization, technical services staff sometimes find their positions being redesigned or possibly eliminated within an automated environment. A few individuals will respond to these circumstances like Melville's Bartleby, who simply and unemotionally stated, "No, at present I would prefer not to make any change at all."[10] These people will need additional encouragement and training if they remain in their positions, or they will become technological casualties who seek jobs more compatible with their personalities than those which now exist in libraries. Other restructuring comes from reduction in professional staff because of attrition followed by a shift in responsibilities to support staff with reclassified job descriptions. Ten years ago Richard Dougherty observed that networks allowed libraries to "reduce gradually the number of professional positions in technical services areas."[11] The reality that original cataloging often takes more time to complete via a bibliographic utility frequently gets overlooked when reductions or reclassifications are needed.

Breaking up tasks previously assigned to one person is sometimes necessary. The process can be threatening unless all involved are open and tactful in their negotiations. Extracting one job assignment from a person and changing it or reassigning it in order to improve the flow of work is a delicate strategy. Unless individuals carefully and continuously assess the impact of automation on their own work and suggest improvements, a few people will soon become overburdened and others relatively idle. Reshaping jobs results in changed staffing patterns and improved workflow. Techniques such as job enlargement, job enrichment, job rotation, or reclassification produce changes in positions.

Job enlargement usually signifies a quantitative increase in duties but may not actually satisfy the person if additional assignments, salary or position upgrade do not follow. Job enrichment offers a change to pursue creative and minimally supervised routines that need to be addressed at a later time. To capitalize on initiative, enthusiasm, and momentum, however, the factor of "later" becomes "now." Unlike job enlargement, job enrichment is temporary and dependent on special projects. Job rotation can increase the workload of two people as each learns the responsibilities of the other.[12] Rotation, unlike enlargement, can prove satisfying, alleviate boredom, and provide essential backup in case of an extended absence.

Job reclassification is the result of job enlargement or position upgrade because of reductions or restructuring in another area. The tedious steps often required for this process command the best communication skills and support. The paperwork and interviews involve several levels of the organizational or university hierarchy. The specific person in the affected position bears equal responsibility in presenting a knowledgeable, rational, and clear response to show how the job has changed to merit reclassification upward.

None of these facets of job reshaping should occur without analysis of each task and the percent of time spent performing that task. Each person can list activities, amount of time spent daily, weekly, or monthly, and discuss the results with the supervisor. The supervisor can then review, transfer, delete or reinforce duties for all staff. Another approach is to have each person write specific tasks on index cards, one item per card. Then in a group setting, the supervisor and staff discuss and arrange tasks in various logical piles based on effective work flow. Separating the person from the activities is often impossible, but frank discussions of jobs and suggested amendments can produce an equitable and improved set of routines.

JOB TRAINING

Whether a library has some automation or a totally integrated system, all staff require training and enhancement of skills. On-site sessions during an implementation period, or prior to installation of equipment provide inexpensive opportunities for initial practice and information about the new system. Vendors usually send a representative to conduct training sessions at little or no additional cost to the library. Long after those early days, however, an incoming employee too often receives hurried, in-house instruction, peruses manuals, or possibly attends local or regional workshops if budget and time are compatible. The growth of users' councils, regional update sessions, issues-oriented seminars and other developmental opportunities benefit all staff in technical services. The value of association with other library personnel who share common goals, systems and problems remains immeasurable.

In addition to refining search strategies, interpreting system messages, and absorbing additional background information about computers, these sessions allow staff to feel mobile and social, not tied to a pneumatic chair preferring not to make any change at all. Reduced mobility is a dissolving myth soon to be supplanted by the reality of increased interdependence of technical services with all areas of the library and with external sources as well. The role of technical services staff magnifies in transforming the bibliographic databases in their coded formats to the user-oriented finished product. The online public access catalogs shield users from the intricate displays of complex transactions accomplished in technical services with human and machine resources. Accountability for data entered correctly and promptly and commitment to quality suddenly thrust staff into a potentially uncomfortable, stressful, and certainly demanding position.

ERGONOMICS

Human nature safely supports the certainty that at some point during each day a library patron or employee will comment on one aspect of the environment. Safety, aesthetics, comfort, noise, quality and condition of equipment, lighting, radiation, and now asbestos exemplify ergonomic factors that compose the physical surroundings of a workplace. Ergonomics is the concept of blending all of these factors with the needs of people and the requirements of machines. Consider the following description of a carefully designed area:

> I placed his desk close up to a small side window in that part of the room, a window which originally had afforded a lateral view of certain grimy backyards and bricks, but which owing to subsequent erections commanded at present no view at all, though it gave some light. Within three feet of the panes was a wall, and the light came down from far above, between two loft buildings, as from a very small opening in a dome. Still

further to a satisfactory arrangement, I procured a high green folding screen, which might entirely isolate Bartleby from my sight, though not remove him from my voice. And thus, in a manner, privacy and society were conjoined.[13]

Melville's description is unfortunately not so very far removed from one we might offer in the twentieth century. With particular interest today in redesigning areas or accommodating computer installations, staff in technical services often wonder what will be moved next. Flexibility upstages necessity as the mother of invention. Except for those few blessed with a budget for new facilities, most libraries must stretch budgets, ideas, and alter the current surroundings to arrive at a suitable atmosphere within which to work, change, and grow.

How many staff sit on secretarial chairs designed in the 1950s? How many fight fluorescent freckles in their frontline of vision after sitting at a computer for a few hours? Who suffers from a sore neck after chasing the elusive entry on a blurry microfiche reader? Suddenly we engage in musical chairs, we appropriate footstools, boxes, or books beneath desks designed for typewriters also belonging to the 1950s; we visit eye doctors, chiropractors, and frequently have hands in aspirin bottles. Although technical services staff are often among the first to attain competency in computer systems, they lack woefully in suitable ergonomic surroundings to match machine progress. Most of us are decades away from being able to agree with Ganga Dakshinamurti, who states, "Obviously libraries are well equipped with chairs that can be adjusted to the needs of individuals."[14]

The components of a quality work station in libraries focus on what employees need in order to complete tasks with a minimum of stress and discomfort and a maximum of effective work. Robert Mason presents some practical ideas concerning human/machine arrangements:

1. Select chairs that give proper height and range of adjustments.
2. Design visual display terminal screens as part of the work area, not just as accessories stuck onto desks.
3. Place visual display terminal keyboards approximately 26" from the floor — conventional writing surfaces are 30" — so that they slope slightly.[15]

In a 1980 survey, Louis Harris and Associates indicated that good lighting and a comfortable chair were the most important factors affecting comfort in a work setting, while the need to work without interruption proved significant too.[16] The Buffalo Organization for Social and Technological Innovation (BOSTI) studied four basic kinds of office environments; open, no partitions; open, separated partitions; open, partitions integrated; and closed. The final BOSTI report, issued in March 1984, suggests that the totally open, bullpen environment is the worst in terms of effective communication and productivity. Areas partitioned above eye level and on three sides allowed easiest communication and best job satisfaction. The BOSTI study specifically noted that in library technical services areas, the concepts of general office design are valid; public services, however, poses different design problems because of dual work spaces for office and patron areas.[17]

Surveys and questionnaires are useful as data points for assessing attitudes towards library work settings and planning for change. Administrators seeking opinions and desiring to base decisions on several pieces of information can benefit from a literature search and simple surveys such as that in Table 1. First administered to a technical services staff at a medium-sized academic library in 1978 by a senior student for an office management project, the survey in Table 1 was later given in 1982 and 1987 to see if attitudes toward the surroundings, especially in view of increased automation, had changed. Responses reflect both faculty and staff attitudes within the department with a total response rate of 88% in 1982 and 84% in 1987.

In fiction Bartleby's employer sought to join privacy and society; in reality we do the same, choosing instead to couch the goals in futuristic terms such as "ergonomics" and "quality of work life." The considerations are the same: we are striving to balance autonomy and interaction, to provide sensible, comfortable surroundings and an atmosphere conducive to accomplishment of library goals.

FINANCIAL RESOURCES

Commitments or constraints? These questioning words concisely define the dilemma library administrators face with financial resources. To be sensitive to all personnel needs and to acquire and maintain quality systems that will provide excellent patron services

Table 1

Questionnaire Concerning Office Environment

	1982 Faculty n=11		1982 Staff n=12		1987 Faculty n=8		1987 Staff n=13	
	Yes	No	Yes	No	Yes	No	Yes	No
1. Do you prefer the present open office concept as opposed to more private areas (partial dividers, plants, etc.)?	27%	63%	58%	41%	25%	75%	46%	38%
2. Do you think that your surrounding work area is large enough for the number of employees within that area?	63%	36%	75%	25%	50%	50%	100%	---
3. Do you think that the location of desks (space plan) of your department follows the work flow?	72%	27%	100%	---	38%	50%	85%	15%
4. Have you found your desk to be suitable for your storage needs?	81%	18%	75%	16%	75%	13%	77%	23%
5. If you had your choice, would you prefer a different type desk?	18%	81%	25%	75%	25%	75%	54%	46%
6. Does your chair give you the physical comfort you need?	100%	---	91%	8%	87%	13%	62%	38%
7. Is the lighting adequate and comfortable for your work area?	72%	27%	82%	18%	87%	13%	92%	8%
8. Do you think there is too much "noise" in your work area that distracts you?	18%	81%	16%	83%	37%	63%	15%	85%
9. Would you prefer that the bells (or ringers) on the telephone be changed?	27%	72%	8%	91%	13%	87%	31%	69%
10. Do you think the office environment would be improved by providing music?	36%	45%	58%	33%	13%	75%	62%	31%
11. Is the temperature in your work area comfortable all year?	---	100%	---	100%	---	100%	15%	85%

demand tough decisions and careful analysis of long-term goals within the context of the university's mission or the community's needs. In "Rocking-Horse Winner" D. H. Lawrence creates a haunting phrase that readily transfers to libraries today, "There must be more money!"[18] To maintain existing operations, to implement future technologies, to reshape jobs and award merit, and to offer training opportunities require money. The strategies, funding, and constraints vary significantly among libraries, but all share the pressures to predict future expenditures, to support ongoing services, and to eliminate or change existing ones.

Trading faculty positions for technical assistants, offering local instead of attending out-of-state workshops, reallocating funds as employees retire or resign are examples of financial alternatives within budgets. Funding is the cornerstone of all of our change today; it too remains a hydra yet to be conquered. We will always face tight budgets and struggle with decisions about services, staff and systems. As Hugh Atkinson succinctly commented, "For the poorer, for the tighter, for the less well supported, not for the more," we will be required to change and at the same time continue to provide new and better services.[19]

Budget reductions threaten staff emotionally and financially resulting in "fewer staff, more work for existing staff, more competition and less cooperation among staff, scant time for participation in goal setting or decision making, and additional responsibilities for which one has little training or interest."[20] A rather dismal effect of such reductions surfaced recently at Olin Library, Washington University, St. Louis, where an outside consultant firm was hired to streamline work and reduce costs. The consultants' brief tenure resulted in staff layoffs, production worksheets, and generally intolerable working conditions.[21] Pressures abound from economic and political indicators of the Information Age and affect all professionals engaged in information services. Approximately sixty-six percent of our GNP comes from knowledge-based industries.[22] A commodity different from all others, information cannot be taken away or used up. Libraries then have to commit human, financial, and technological resources to compete with other organizations and businesses for information storage and retrieval, the very nature of technical services units.

TECHNOTHERAPY: Rx FOR STRESS

Similar to the mythological Sisyphus, we are all compelled to roll the technological stone of progress up the hill of the future only to have it topple, forcing us to regroup, push upward once more, and have determination that our goals will be reached. Sisyphus certainly knew what stress meant. We do also. Any one or a combination of factors mentioned earlier is a potential stress point: financial resources, work surroundings, colleagues, computers, communications, and decisions. What appears to be the greatest stressor is loss of interpersonal relationships. We rebel against turning into nerds, noids, or nodes. Brod views technostress as "a modern disease of adaptation caused by inability to cope with the new computer technologies in a healthy manner."[23] If we accept by now that change is stability, then we also admit that librarianship is stressful. What we need not contend with or contribute to is unreasonable or unnecessarily bad climates for accomplishing our job responsibilities. The Orwellian idea of monitoring citizens everywhere and the 1987 attempt to apply production line techniques to library operations fall into that category of unreasonableness.

Technotherapy, in an innocuous and certainly nonclinical sense, simply gives credence to the necessity of considering staff resources, physical environment, unit goals, and constantly reassessing all the components of an automated environment. There should be little occasion for the more drastic outlet of clinical sessions if we are willing to risk new styles of solving issues within changed settings. If staff can recognize stress inherent in each new process and discuss concerns freely, knowing that they will be listened to, then tensions, real or potential, can dissipate. The emerging nature of successful technical services units cuts through stratified layers of communication and seeks the challenge of openness and understanding of shared responsibility. This spirit of cooperation and willingness will bridge each new technological gap.

Shirley Leung recommends the following ways of coping with any frustrating situation:

1. Know yourself and your environment.
2. Set priorities and choose the right thing to do at the right time.
3. Develop a system of social support.
4. Try not to take things personally.
5. Be open.
6. Find an occupation and environment most compatible with your own personality.[24]

A sense of humor and flexibility also serve well in alleviating stress. Laughing at another title change in a serial or the receipt of a Diner's Club application for Ms. Helm-Cravens Executive certainly services the psyche better than agitation and mutterings about the impersonal messages of computers.

WANTED: INNOVATIVE PARTNERSHIPS

Whatever our role in technical services, we are all thinkers, planners, and doers. We each have a left side and right side to our brains. The connection between those halves makes it possible to develop manual dexterity for data input and logical skills to analyze and provide explanations for what we have entered. Future changes in technical services will come from innovative practices that affect daily routines. Complacency no longer fits in a library undergoing technological transition. Charles Martell remarks that our challenge is to move from the business of circulating books and maintaining card files to the explosive practice of providing information and access to it in a multitude of forms.[25] We cannot continue to let change affect us; we must effect change. To concentrate on the best ways to blend technology and personnel needs and to encourage every person to develop many skills is the challenge for the next decade. Martell underscores the basic tenet that evolved when computers first arrived in libraries: "People are the key resource, not as instruments but as foundations upon which creativity, initiative, and progress are built."[26] Communication, involvement, and innovation represent the emphasis needed to capitalize on human resources in a positive way. Computers are commonplace; people never are.

NOTES

1. Rhoda Thomas Tripp, Comp. *The International Thesaurus* (New York: Thomas Y. Crowell, 1970), p. 74.

2. Craig Brod, *Technostress: The Human Cost of the Computer Revolution* (Reading, MA: Addison Wesley, 1984), p. 16.

3. Brod, 53.

4. Shirley W. Leung, "Coping With Stress: A Technical Services Perspective," *Journal of Library Administration* 5 (Spring 1984):15.

5. Rosabeth Moss Center. *The Change Masters* (New York: Simon, 1983), p. 41.

6. Henriette D. Avram, "Overview—The Impact of Technology on Libraries," *IFLA Journal* 10 (1984):26.

7. Canter, p. 122.

8. Thomas Blakeslee, *The Right Brain: A New Understanding of Our Unconscious Mind and Its Creative Power* (Garden City, NY: Doubleday, 1980), p. 6.

9. Grace Bulaong, "Man and Machine: Staff Adaptation to Library Automation," *Ontario Library Review* 66 (June 1982):39.

10. Herman Melville, "Bartleby the Scrivener," *The Portable Melville*, ed. Jay Leyda (New York: Viking, 1952), p. 506.

11. Richard M. Dougherty, "Personnel Needs for Librarianship's Uncertain Future," *Academic Libraries by the Year 2000*, ed. Herbert Poole (New York: Bowker, 1977), p. 107.

12. A. Cakir, D. J. Hart and T. F. M. Stewart, *Visual Display Terminals* (New York: Wiley and Sons, 1980), p. 243.

13. Melville, p. 475.

14. Ganga Dakshinamurti, "Automation's Effect on Library Personnel," *Canadian Library Journal* 42 (December 1985):346.

15. Robert Mason, "Ergonomics: The Human and the Machine," *Library Journal* 109.3 (Feb. 15, 1984):331-332.

16. Jeanne M. Isacco, "Work Spaces, Satisfaction, and Productivity in Libraries," *Library Journal* 110.8 (May 1, 1985):28.

17. Isacco, p. 29-30.

18. D. H. Lawrence, "The Rocking Horse Winner," *The Tales of D. H. Lawrence* (London: Secker, 1934), p. 968.

19. Hugh C. Atkinson, "Strategies for Change: Part I," *Library Journal* 109.1 (Jan. 1984):59.

20. Mary Haack, John W. Jones, and Tina Roose, "Occupational Burnout Among Librarians," *Drexel Library Quarterly* 20 (Spring 1984):66.

21. Art Plotnik, "Kicking Librarian Butt," *American Libraries* 18.4 (April 1987):236.

22. Avram, p. 25.

23. Brod, p. 16.

24. Leung, p. 17.

25. Charles Martell, "QWL Strategies; People Are the Castle, People Are the Walls, People Are the Moat," *Journal of Academic Librarianship* 10 (1984):354.

26. Martell, p. 350.

REFERENCES

Allan, Ann, and Kathy J. Reynolds. "Performance Problems: A Model for Analysis and Resolution." *Journal of Academic Librarianship* 9 (May 1983):83-88.

Cohen, Elaine, and Aaron Cohen. *Automation, Space Management, and Productivity: A Guide for Libraries*. New York: Bowker, 1982.

Conroy, Barbara, and Barbara Schindler Jones. *Improving Communication in the Library*. Phoenix, AZ: Oryx, 1986.

Cooper, Cary L., and Roy Payne, eds. *Concurrent Concerns in Occupational Stress*. New York: Wiley and Sons, 1980.

Decker, Jean S. "QWL in Academic/Research Libraries." *Technical Services Quarterly* 3 (Fall 1985/Winter 1985-86):51-58.

Fine, Sara F. "Technological Innovation, Diffusion, and Resistance: An Historical Perspective." *Journal of Library Administration* 7 (Spring 1986):83-108.

Freedman, Maurice J. "Automation and the Future of Technical Services." *Library Journal* 109 (June 15, 1984):1197-1203.

Friedman, Fred T. "Something There Is That Doesn't Love a Computer (Nor Hate It Either)." *Library Journal* 109 (June 15, 1984):1190-1193.

Henshaw, Rod. "Library to Library." *Wilson Library Bulletin* 60 (April 1986): 44-45.

Kent, Allen, and Thomas J. Galvin. *Information Technology: Critical Choices for Library Decision-Makers*. New York: Marcel Dekker, 1982.

Malinconico, S. Michael. "People and Machines: Changing Relationships?" *Library Journal* 108 (December 1, 1983):2222-2224.

Manning, Leslie A. "Technical Services Administration." In *Library Technical Services, Operations and Management*, pp. 15-42. Edited by Irene P. Godden. Orlando, FL: Academic, 1984.

Martell, Charles. "Investing in People." *Journal of Academic Librarianship* 9 (March 1983):33-35.

———. "The Nature of Authority and Employee Participation in the Management of Academic Libraries." *College and Research Libraries* 48 (March 1987):110-122.

Repp, Joan M. "The Response of the Cataloger and the Catalog to Automation in the Library Setting." In *Advances in Library Administration and Organization*, v. 5, pp. 67-89. Edited by Gerard McCabe and Bernard Kreissman. Greenwich, CT: JAI, 1986.

Sack, John R. "Open Systems for Open Minds: Building the Library Without Walls." *College and Research Libraries*. 47 (November 1986):535-544.

Smith, Michael J., Barbara G. F. Cohen, and Lambert W. Stammerjohn. "An Investigation of Health Complaints and Job Stress in Video Display Operations." *Human Factors* 23 (August 1981):387-400.

Taylor, David C. *Managing the Serials Explosion, the Issues for Publishers and Libraries*. New York: Knowledge Industry, 1982.

Torok, Andrew G. "Ergonomics Considerations in Microcomputing." *Microcomputers for Information Management* 1 (September 1984):229-250.

White, Herbert S. *Library Personnel Management*. White Plains, NY: Knowledge Industry, 1985.

Yglesias, Donna B. "Improving Staff Creativity, Productivity and Accountability." In *Austerity Management in Academic Libraries*, pp. 255-268. Edited by John F. Harvey and Peter Spyers-Duran. Metuchen, NJ: Scarecrow, 1984.

Staffing Technical Services in 1995

Janet Swan Hill

Of forces affecting libraries today, the two strongest, automation and money,[1] have an especially direct impact on technical services. Because many technical services tasks are repetitive, they were an early focus of library automation.[2] Because technical services operations account for a large portion of library personnel budgets, and their products are countable,[3] they are an obvious object for administrative scrutiny.[4] Both automation and cost containment will remain important until 1995 and beyond,[5] influencing the work that technical services does, its size, its shape, and the nature of its staff.

Some predictions for technical services have been made so often that they have come close to being thought inevitable (e.g., the "blurring of lines" between technical and public services).[6,7] Others are made so frequently that the extent to which they are already true is obscured (e.g., the separation of original and copy cataloging).[8] Some forecasts have turned out to be wrong, such as De Gennaro's 1970s conviction that cataloging was a specialty nearing extinction.[9] Others will be at least significantly delayed, such as Lancaster's belief that libraries' replacement of locally-owned printed materials in favor of remote electronic information sources will eliminate the need for local processing.[10] Adding to the confusion is the fact that predictions are often phrased as if all types and sizes of libraries had the same needs and capacities and responded identically to the same developments.

Freedman has observed that librarians have a propensity for being overoptimistic in projecting expectations for the future based on a few questionably applicable successes,[11] and until recently, li-

Janet Swan Hill is Head, Catalog Department, Northwestern University Library, Evanston, IL.

braries' experience with automation was so limited that guesses were all that was possible.[12] Reports of longer experience are at last beginning to appear,[13] however, to assist librarians in making their guesses better informed.

STAFFING: WHAT'S INVOLVED

Even if the direction of library automation and technological development were known absolutely, no single prediction about technical services staffing would serve all libraries; no magic formula relating the materials budget or volumes added to the number or type of staff can be determined. Even a group of libraries that are similar in many ways, the Association of Research Libraries (ARL) members, exhibit no such consistent relationships.[14] If a formula were developed, it would still not illuminate the skills requirements for positions. Major variables affecting libraries and staff, however, can be identified. These include: what technical services encompasses; how technical services functions are organized; and how the nature of the work is changing. These factors are themselves influenced by the size of a library's staff, the nature of its collection, the automation options chosen, and the stage of implementation.

WHAT DOES TECHNICAL SERVICES ENCOMPASS?

However a library is organized, the work to be done can be divided into two types: technical services functions are process-oriented and focused on making library materials available to information seekers. They include a substantial concentration of activities, are focused on library users, and involve actions that are less typically repetitive or codifiable. It is important to remember that this categorization applies to the work, not to the people.[15] An understanding of both types of work must inform all operations.

The traditional technical services functions include cataloging and acquisitions. Two other functions are increasingly listed. Circulation, sitting at the interface between materials and users, has usually been considered part of public services, but automation has emphasized its repetitive aspects, and integrated systems are revealing kinship between circulation and cataloging information. Preservation, increasingly important especially in research libraries, can be considered an augmentation to binding or mending. These potential alliances are acknowledged, but neither function is covered in this paper.

HOW ARE TECHNICAL SERVICES FUNCTIONS ORGANIZED?

Possible futures envisioned for technical services organization have ranged from nonexistence, through no essential change, to expansion. Lancaster forecasts a library-less state by 2001, in which "organization and control" activities will be performed centrally rather than at individual libraries.[16] Atkinson and Gorman, through publications about "ecumenical librarians,"[17] "tribal" organization,[18] and "doing away with technical services departments"[19] have advocated decentralization of technical services within a library, pointing out that remote access to files via computer makes such a plan feasible. They have been careful to note that regardless of structure, the functions still have to be performed, and that for some nonprofessional duties centralization may still be best.[20] Among advantages claimed for dispersal of professional staff are increased job satisfaction, greater mobility and promotability,[21,22] enhanced status[23] and greater ease of meeting tenure requirements.[24] Freedman believes that professional control is not easily distributed, and suggests that only tasks that "do not require specific expertise or supervision" be dispersed.[25] The reality is that although many libraries have made organizational changes in response to automation,[26] "institutional inertia"[27] remains a powerful force. A 1984 survey of ARL members revealed little integration of technical services with other library functions.[28] Many small libraries, however, have so few librarians that no other model is feasible.[29] There are four basic patterns that may be seen in libraries, each of which has certain characteristic effects on staff:

A. Larger libraries, centralized technical services. Centralized technical services operations became commonplace about thirty years ago,[30] and will remain a common pattern for some time to come. Except for administrators, jobs are narrowly focused, and skills are developed and exercised over relatively small segments of the operation. Changes in number and classification of staff derive most directly from changes in the amount and type of work to be done, which are in turn determined by local and network automation decisions, and by materials acquisition and staff budgets.

B. *Larger libraries, technical services dispersed.* The most likely configuration for dispersal includes distribution of professional functions to branches and collections, but continued centralization of most nonprofessional activities. Classification levels at the central node are lower than in the branches, nonprofessional jobs are narrowly focused, and professional positions are managerial. Changes in number and level of staff are determined as for A above. Dispersal of professional duties, on the other hand, divides a library system into a number of smaller entities that behave as if they were self-contained small libraries. Librarians need to be competent in a range of activities, they must be aware of all aspects of librarianship, and must constantly balance the needs of departmental clientele against requirements for the system as a whole. The smaller the entities and the greater their number, the greater the potential for inefficiencies and inconsistencies that arise from doing a complex job part time, and from having less consultative access to other professionals doing similar work.[31]

C. *Smaller libraries, technical services retained.* Smaller libraries that perform most of their own technical services function (libraries with specialized collections, those unaffiliated with a central processing unit, etc.) will continue to need staff for technical services activities, although the amount of time required should gradually decrease. Staff must be responsible for several phases of operations, and are likely not to be limited to technical services tasks only. Where there is too little work, or too few staff to assign work at appropriate levels, a librarian may perform some nonprofessional duties, or a nonprofessional may be asked to do work for which she or he is not completely qualified.

D. *Smaller libraries, technical services performed elsewhere.* Many small, nonspecialized libraries (e.g., public or school branches with centralized processing), will be able to cede most technical services operations to a central entity, and will need a very small staff component to accomplish the processing steps left to be done locally.[32] Processing policy decisions will usually be made at the central facility. Local staff with technical services duties will be "multi-purpose" within the library. Training and problem solving will increasingly require interaction of staff from all libraries in the system.[33]

HOW IS THE NATURE OF TECHNICAL
SERVICES WORK CHANGING?

Bibliographic Networks

Libraries have been using externally supplied cataloging to enhance productivity for most of this century. If bibliographic networks simply made copy more readily available, their impact on library operations would be beneficial, but would have involved no essential change in the role of individual libraries. By enabling libraries to add to the central store of shared cataloging records, networks have fostered copy availability to the point where many libraries need never catalog a title from scratch, and even large libraries have only a small portion of titles that require original cataloging. Use and contribution of shared copy require that libraries adhere to common standards over which they may have little influence. For libraries that use a network acquisitions system, the same limits to local flexibility apply to acquisitions. The cost is one that most libraries consider more than offset by the benefits.

Automation (Other Than Bibliographic Networks)

Library automation continues to enable increased efficiency and speed in technical services. Automation implementation is the impetus for abandonment or simplification of many complex practices (e.g., filing rules, customized cross references, etc.), but for virtually every operation simplified, some other activity becomes more complex. Thus, while some tasks now take fewer or no staff (e.g., serials claiming, card filing), other operations are more complicated (e.g., cataloging), or have taken on increased significance (e.g., authority control). Some services that used to be essentially impossible to provide (e.g., off-site catalogs), are feasible with automation, and staff freed from one task may be retrained to perform new functions.

De Gennaro argues that savings in unskilled labor are more than offset by increases in skilled work, and that computer systems mainly lead to exchanges of one kind of position for another, including movement for positions from libraries to networks.[34] Northwestern's experience suggests that automation leads to fewer technical services staff at the highest and lowest levels, and to slightly fewer staff in the middle range, but the staff in the middle will have to be more skilled and better trained than before.[35]

Although automation may appear to be inevitable to librarians in large and medium-sized libraries, Edgar reminds us of the many small and underfunded libraries across the nation for which automation may be out of reach for some time.[36]

Retrospective Conversion (Recon)

As libraries convert catalog records from card to machine-readable form, they experience a temporary addition to their workload. Possible approaches to conversion are many and have varied impacts on staffing. Recon can be accomplished by staff hired for the purpose, temporarily swelling technical services. Conversion can take temporary precedence over current cataloging,[37] requiring few or no additional staff, but leaving an accumulation of postponed cataloging to be dealt with after the project is completed. Recon can be done very slowly, eking work out of staff already on hand, in which case any staff added may be so few as to be almost unnoticeable, and may simply be turned to other tasks as soon as conversion is complete. The state and type of a particular library's conversion effort will determine how many of what types of staff will be on hand in 1995.

Professional Staff

A simplified distinction between professional and nonprofessional staff is that professionals make judgments, while nonprofessionals follow rules. As bibliographic networks and other external databases expand, and as automation imposes standardization on an increasing number of technical services operations, the body of work over which judgment must be exercised is shrinking. As technological developments enable increased speed and efficiency in nonprofessional tasks, the number of staff needing professional supervision decreases. But handling individual items, managing workflow, and supervising staff are not the only tasks that call for professional training and perspective. Policies and practices must keep pace with evolving technologies. The planning to enable libraries to shape the future to their needs, and themselves to the future requires committed and informed librarians with a full understanding and appreciation of what goes on in technical services, accompanied by an awareness of the interrelatedness of all library functions in pursuit of the common goal of serving users.

TECHNICAL SERVICES FUNCTIONS

Acquisitions

Materials selection and acquisitions processing can be performed by a single unit or person. Increasingly, however, in libraries large enough to divide the work, acquisitions is defined as consisting only of processing, and selection is performed by librarians outside technical services.[38] Most acquisitions processing tasks do not require professional judgment, and virtually all aspects of ordering, receiving, checking-in and claiming can be performed by support staff.[39] Librarians in an acquisitions processing department will perform predominantly administrative functions, including supervision, planning, policy development, and monitoring expenditures and vendor performance.[40] Except in large libraries, a single librarian or part of a librarian, will be sufficient. Alley suggests that an acquisitions manager may not need to be a librarian at all so long as she or he is qualified in purchasing and accounting, and is willing to learn library terminology.[41] In the fifteen years since Northwestern's technical processing functions were automated, the greatest decrease in professional staff has been in acquisitions.[42]

As automation is increasingly applied to acquisitions, both time and number of support staff will be reduced through elimination or translation of manual routines such as filing, sorting, record keeping, and claiming.[43] Interactive access to network, vendor, and publisher databases will enable capture of data, eliminating the error-prone rekeying process, and eventually reducing the need to print and mail orders and claims.[44] Almost all jobs will involve computers, ranging from data input to database searching, to manipulation of computer programs such as accounting and statistical analysis packages. Typing—and accuracy will be essential. "Computer literacy" will be important for some jobs.

Some cataloging functions may shift into acquisitions. Bibliographic copy obtained from a network can in some instances be edited for local use at point of item receipt, bypassing the catalog department.[45] Integration of automation applications offers the possibility for acquisitions to perform both pre-order and pre-cataloging searching in one step,[46] and to pass the online results directly to cataloging. Staff who do these tasks must be more highly trained than those whose work "stops at the border," especially if the work displays in the catalog as a preliminary record or a finished product. Not only must they master more steps and techniques, they must also have an understanding of cataloging conventions and catalog use.

The benefits of acquisitions automation are not all in the realm of improving nonprofessional productivity in existing duties. Data generated through automated operations can also be used to perform tasks always desirable, but essentially unattainable, such as routine vendor performance studies. The design of such mechanisms and interpretation of their results are professional activities whose importance will increase as the problems of selecting materials and optimizing fund allocations grow in complexity with shrinking budgets and new forms of library materials.[47] Larger libraries that resist the trend to denude acquisitions of professionals will have reason to feel pleased with their decision, and the librarians that remain will have jobs that are at once more demanding and more interesting than before. It will no longer be enough for them to understand the operational mechanisms of accounting and purchasing, nor even to have supervisory skills. Awareness of technological developments, imagination to see their possible impacts, and willingness to plan and experiment, combined with the ability to use modern tools (computers, software packages, etc.) to analyze trends and possible actions will be increasingly important.

Cataloging

Cataloging is one of the most expensive library operations, often occupying more librarians and support staff than any other unit. Despite its centrality to the profession, however, cataloging may be the operation most foreign to other librarians.[48] Automation was applied to cataloging relatively early, with bibliographic networks at first concentrating almost entirely on cataloging functions. Assisted by automation, cataloging departments have increased productivity, and reduced their staff. Unfortunately, once the easy savings derived from copy use, nonredundancy of entry, ease of correction, etc. have been realized, further cost reduction mechanisms are slower to identify, less spectacular in yield, and require compromises, such as uniform acceptance of LC practice, and decreased revision of shared copy. Many administrators find a slowed pace of improvement frustrating. Some begin to question the value of cataloging and its component parts, casting catalogers as villains in the piece, using "perfection" as a pejorative term,[49,50] and redefining "accuracy" and "productivity" as antonyms.

Cataloging provides the clearest instance of technology-born deprofessionalization of library functions,[51] but it is necessary to remember that what has changed is not the professional nature of original cataloging, but rather the amount of original cataloging there is to do. Confusion on this point may arise from using the term "cataloging" to describe two activities. Failure to distinguish between "cataloging" and "copy cataloging" may lead to inappropriate decisions, just as failure to distinguish between "skis" and "water skis" might lead to an accident or embarrassment. Describing and analyzing library materials from scratch required professional education and judgment. Editing pre-existing copy for local use does not, and there is now enough copy available from the Library of Congress and networks, that depending on their size and collecting patterns, most libraries can obtain copy for 80-100% of their titles.[54,55] Thus, to the extent that a library's acquisitions have copy available, some professional cataloging positions can be abolished, and replaced by nonprofessionals. The ratio of new to old positions depends on the extent to which librarians performed copy cataloging and the speed of copy cataloging relative to original cataloging.

If, for instance, a title with copy can be handled in 15 minutes, while a title cataloged originally requires one hour, and if usable copy is found for 80% of titles, then two professional catalogers can handle 2,000 titles in 400 hours. If items without copy are separated from those with copy, 2,000 titles can be done in 400 hours by one librarian and one paraprofessional. The number of staff does not decrease, but the payroll does. If the hit rate is 95%, two librarians can handle 2,000 titles in 49% less time (237.5 hours). Those same titles can be handled in the same time by 0.4 librarians and 1.6 copy catalogers. In general, the larger or more specialized the library, the lower the hit rate and the smaller the relative reduction in staff numbers and payroll. Smaller less specialized libraries may enjoy sizeable reductions in numbers and costs. Some may be able to dispense with professional catalogers altogether, either through a 100% hit rate, or through contracting out for cataloging.[52] Many libraries, of course, have already experienced these changes. For them the near future promises gradual improvement as hit rates creep upward, local processing is streamlined, and automation extends its boundaries.

The classification level appropriate for copy catalogers can be debated. Some authors insist that increased standardization will enable use of less skilled workers,[53] while others note that automation makes the work more complex,[54] generating a general shift upward in classification.[55] Both views may be correct. Copy that is essentially accepted as it comes can be handled by support staff at relatively low classification levels. When copy is more thoroughly scrutinized, or if it must be substantially altered, more highly-trained paraprofessionals are required.[56] Either type of staff will need typing and input skills, computer familiarity, and accuracy. Copy catalogers who are expected to assess correctness of tagging or cataloging, to verify, construct, or complete call numbers, or to establish headings for local use must acquire all those skills, and must also be led to a realization of the overall framework into which their work fits. Intner suggests that a cost-effective way to provide some of this training is to send them to library school classes, where along with specific skills, they will also be exposed to the principles and purposes of the work.[57]

The continued success of copy cataloging depends on continuation of original cataloging, since someone must first prepare copy later utilized by paraprofessionals. Unfortunately, automation's impact on original cataloging has been marginal, and although future developments may enhance catalogers' ability to handle individual titles,[58] the intellectual decisions that make original cataloging an art remain.[59] Some are called into play more often, since corner-cutting was common when records were used only locally, but participation in a bibliographic network substantially precludes such tactics.[60] Automation also adds layers of detail and decisions not previously part of the cataloging process, calling for greater expertise on the part of original catalogers,[61,62] and tending to reduce their productivity.

Other factors that mitigate against imminent obsolescence for cataloging librarians include the growth of NACO, a cooperative project for building the national authority file, and eventually a national bibliographic database, that relies heavily on expert professional catalogers across the country;[63] the increasingly esoteric nature of items left without copy;[64] potential cooperative agreements whereby libraries assume responsibility for cataloging titles from collections in which they are preeminent; and expansion of cataloging activities to materials previously shortchanged (e.g., maps, government publications, archival materials, newspapers), as well as to new formats (e.g., compact disks, videotapes, computer files).

Professional library degree programs cannot possibly provide everything a cataloger needs to know. Library automation, information technology, and the possible formats of information resources are moving targets. Cataloging librarians will need a grasp of cataloging principles and basic rules that is firm enough to enable intelligent application of those principles to the circumstances of the day. The decline in relative numbers of English language materials without copy, and the decreasing number of catalogers among whom to spread subject fields will make foreign language competencies and a general breadth of knowledge increasingly important, except where catalogers serve specialized collections. An understanding of automation, especially as it relates to network operations[65] will assist catalogers in day-to-day work, in designing effective work strategies, and in interracting with network personnel. And even professionals must know how to type. The advice given to Lucia Rather by her father can no longer be confidently followed.[66]

Catalog departments do more than produce bibliographic records. They also produce and manage the catalog itself. With increasing automation of the processes and product of cataloging, "catalog management" will evolve into "database management" and may increase in size.[67] Authority work will be more complex, and the consequences of not performing it more serious. Online catalogs, especially union catalogs, call for strict heading consistency and control, and although the main work of heading and reference formulation may or may not remain with individual catalogers, oversight and maintenance of the file itself will no longer be an invisible function, but a separate activity, perhaps overseen by a librarian.[68] Maintenance of the catalog as a whole will also undergo metamorphosis. "Database correction," involving computer input and invocation of global changes, calls for a different level of staff than "catalog correction," which was suitably staffed by clerks armed with erasers and correction fluid. Card filing, on the other hand, may soon require no staff at all.[69]

Any large operation needs to be managed. In times of rapid change, effective management is crucial. Librarians will need to plan, supervise, and coordinate the multiple activities that result in the creation of a catalog,[70] to help their institutions make the best use of future developments, and to guide those developments to meet the needs of the institution. Cataloging knowledge alone will not be enough for these positions, even if accompanied by supervisory skills. An understanding of principles underlying the field as a whole is also necessary. Cataloging managers will need to follow technological developments, and to make a habit of speculating about how they might affect operations. They will need to know the techniques of planning, "futuring," and experimentation, including application of relevant computer packages to those activities.

Materials Processing

Machine-produced labels for library materials have been available through some bibliographic networks for years and can also be produced by some local library systems. Whether a label is machine-produced by a network or locally, staff hours involved in matching and affixing labels (in the case of local production) are substantially reduced, and the work requires less review, since the computer does not make typographical or transcription errors. So long as the machine record is correct, the label will also be correct.

Mending will remain essentially unautomated, and the need for it may increase as paper and bindings deteriorate. Unless a library decided not to bind items, or to retain serials back issues in surrogate form (e.g., microform, laser disk, etc.), nonpreservation binding activity will continue. Record keeping will be enhanced by extension of library automation into bindery management.[71] Bindery staff will track materials through an automated system, modifying records already part of the database. The workload will decrease. Job classification will remain the same.

EDUCATION AND RECRUITMENT

No matter how sophisticated a library's automation applications, how distinguished its collection, or how large its acquisition budget, without an adequate number of well-trained, appropriately classified staff carrying out technical services functions, the library will fall short of fulfilling its mission to provide users with understandable, useful, and usable physical and intellectual access to the items it holds (and increasingly to items it has access to). In general, finding and training nonprofessional staff is a problem for the library alone. The supply and preparation of librarians is a matter with less localized impact.

The problem of finding librarians for technical services has recently received considerable attention. A 1985 survey revealed widespread difficulty in filling cataloging vacancies. An inspection of library school curricula discovered relatively thin offerings in cataloging, in technical services as a whole, and especially in acquisitions.[72] Owing partly to the brevity of degree programs, and partly to philosophical conviction, technical services courses that are taught tend to be general and theoretical in nature, making lengthy on-the-job training necessary.[73,74]

Both curricular shortcomings and the dearth of applicants may spring from a misconception that automation will bring about a decimation of technical services, including near extinction of catalogers and acquisitions librarians. But the decrease of professional positions has been gradual, and is likely to remain so.[75] Technical services librarians are still needed, and their role has broadened. Those that remain must be better prepared than ever before in specific technical expertise, in awareness of library issues, and in management techniques.[76,77] Quality education is crucial, perhaps especially in libraries with only one degreed librarian in technical services.[78] Just what form that education should take is unclear. Specialization by function, rather than by type of library has strong proponents,[79,80] as does education that emphasizes the "seamlessness" of librarianship.[81] Whatever the approach taken, library programs are so short, and the field so wide that on-the-job training will always be necessary,[82] although internships, "apprenticeships"[83] or closer association with working libraries[84] might lessen the training period. New librarians hired as the only cataloger or technical services professional in a library have to train themselves. Unfortunately for them and for their libraries, the ease and completeness of that training usually reflects the experience of the teacher.

Nothing stands still. Library automation systems, information technologies, publishing practices, cataloging standards, network operations, library administrations and staff, even foreign exchange rates are constantly changing. The knowledge acquired and techniques mastered during an academic program and professional orientation are not enough to carry technical services librarians through a career. Continuing and supplementary education should be part of every librarian's plan, and part of every library's plans for its staff.

Technical services remains labor intensive regardless of widespread automation. Shrewd selection and implementation of computer hardware and software can enable reduced unit costs. Intelligent work organization and realistic job classification can increase productivity. Regardless of streamlined procedures, regardless of the speed of computers, work remains to be done, and some of it fully justifies professional attention. Libraries spend hundreds of thousands of dollars annually in designing systems, in purchasing hardware and software packages. But in the end, a library's most important resource is its people,[85] and the most important thing about them is not their numbers. Careful selection, appropriate assignment, adequate education, effective training, and continuing support will repay a library in productivity, creativity, and effectiveness.

NOTES

1. Gorman, Michael. "The Ecumenical Librarian," *The Reference Librarian* 9 (Fall/Winter 1983):56.

2. Edgar, Neal L. "Technical Services in Ten Years," *Technical Services Quarterly* 1 (Fall/Winter 1983):12.

3. Holley, Robert P. "The Future of Catalogers and Cataloging," *Journal of Academic Librarianship* 7 (1981):90.

4. Brown, Thomas M. "Technical Services in the 1980s in School Libraries: Trends and Problems," *Illinois Libraries* 62 (1980): 594.

5. Grams, Theodore C. W. "Technical Services: The Decade Ahead," *Technical Services Quarterly* 1 (Fall/Winter 1983):19.

6. Ladd, Dorothy P. "Sharing Staff for Development and Improved Service," *Technical Services Quarterly* 2 (Spring/Summer 1985):121.

7. Gorman, Michael. "Technical Services, 1984-2001 (and Before)," *Technical Services Quarterly* 1 (Fall/Winter 1983):69.

8. Oyler, Patricia G. "Education for Technical Services in the 1980s," *Illinois Libraries* 62 (1980):597.

9. De Gennaro, Richard. "Libraries & Networks in Transition: Problems and Prospects for the 1980's," *Library Journal* 106 (1981):1047.

10. Lancaster, F. W. *Libraries and Librarians in an Age of Electronics.* (Arlington, VA: Information Resources, 1982), pp. 152, 167.

11. Freedman, Maurice J. "Automation and the Future of Technical Services," *Library Journal* 109 (1984):1197.

12. Preston, Gregor A. "How Will Automation Affect Cataloging Staff?" *Technical Services Quarterly* 1 (Fall/Winter 1983):130.

13. Horny, Karen L. "Fifteen Years of Automation: Evolution of Technical

Services Staffing," *Library Resources & Technical Services* 31 (Jan-Mar 1987): 69-76.

14. As indicated by comparison of figures from *ARL Statistics, 1984-85: A Compilation of Statistics From the One Hundred and Eighteen Members of the Association of Research Libraries*. Compiled by Nicola Daval and Alexander Lichtenstein (Washington: ARL, 1986), and the *ARL Supplementary Statistics, 1948 [sic]-85*. Compiled by Robert E. Molyneux (Washington: ARL, 1986).

15. Gorman, "Doing Away With Technical Services Department," p. 437.

16. Lancaster, *Librarians in an Age of Electronics*, pp. 152, 167.

17. Gorman, "Ecumenical Librarian," pp. 55-64.

18. Atkinson, Hugh C. "The Impact of Closing the Catalog on Library Organization," in *Closing the Catalog: Proceedings of the 1978-79 LITA Institutes* (Phoenix: Oryx, 1980), p. 126.

19. Gorman, Michael. "On Doing Away with Technical Services Departments," *American Libraries* 10 (1979):435-437.

20. Gorman, Michael. "Online Access and Organization and Administration of Libraries," in *Online Catalogs, Online Reference, Converging Trends*. (Chicago: ALA, 1984), p. 159.

21. Gorman, "Doing Away with Technical Services Departments," p. 435.

22. Godden, Irene P. *Library Technical Services: Operations and Management*. (Orlando, FL: Academic Press, 1984), p. 7.

23. Bachus, Edward J. "I'll Drink to That: The Integration of Technical and Reader Services," *Journal of Academic Librarianship* 8 (1982):227.

24. Holley, "Future of Catalogs," p. 92.

25. Freedman, "Future of Technical Services," p. 1202.

26. Spyers-Duran, Peter. "The Effects of Automation on Organizational Change, Staffing, and Human Relations in Catalog Departments," in *Requiem for the Card Catalog: Management Issues in Automated Cataloging*. Ed. by Daniel Gore, Joseph Kimbrough and Peter Spyers-Duran. (Westport, CT: Greenwood, 1978), p. 31.

27. Ghikas, Mary W. "Technical Services in the '80's: Challenge and Change," *Illinois Libraries* 62 (1980):589.

28. Association of Research Libraries, Office of Management Studies *Automation and Reorganization of Technical and Public Services* Spec kit 112. (Washington: ARL, 1985), cover sheet.

29. Gorman, "Doing Away With Technical Services Departments," p. 437.

30. Bachus, "I'll Drink to That," p. 260.

31. Peele, David. "Staffing the Reference Desk," *Library Journal* 106, (1980):1711.

32. Adcock, Donald C. "Into the 80s: An Overview of the Future of Technical Services in the School Library," *Illinois Libraries* 62 (1980):592.

33. Funk, Carla and Lizbeth Bishoff. "By Any Name; The Future of Technical Services in the Small and Medium-Sized Libraries," *Illinois Libraries* 62 (1980):591.

34. De Gennaro, "Libraries & Networks in Transition," pp. 1048-1049.

35. Horny, "Fifteen Years of Automation," p. 74.

36. Edgar, "Technical Services in Ten Years," pp. 13, 17.

37. The University of Illinois at Chicago used this approach. (From remarks

delivered at a joint Northwestern/University of Chicago/UIC Professional Development Program by Nancy R. John, February, 1987.)

38. Johnson, Herbert F. "Case Study: Restructuring Technical Services at Emory," *Journal of Academic Librarianship* 9 (1983):34.

39. Gorman, "Online Access," p. 159.

40. High, Walter M. "The role of the Professional in Technical Services," *RTSD Newsletter* 11 (1986):59.

41. Alley, B. "Staffing Technical Services: Expectation vs Realities" *Illinois Libraries* 67 (1985):482.

42. Horny, "Fifteen Years of Automation," pp. 71, 74.

43. Harrington, Sue Anne. "The Changing Environment in Technical Services" *Technical Services Quarterly* 4 (Winter 1986):12.

44. Aveney, Brian and Luba Heinemann. "Acquisitions and Collection Development Automation: Future Directions," *Library Hi Tech* 1 (Summer 1983):47.

45. Horny, Karen L. "Automation: The Context and the Potential," in *Library Technical Services: Operations and Management*. (Orlando, FL: Academic Press, 1984), p. 47.

46. Horny, "Fifteen Years of Automation," p. 71.

47. Lancaster, *Librarians in an Age of Electronics*, p. 94.

48. Hyman, Richard J. *Urban Academic Librarian* 5 (Fall/Winter, 1986/87):35-38.

49. Hafter, Ruth. *Academic Librarians and Cataloging Networks: Visibility, Quality Control, and Professional Status*. Contributions in Librarianship and Information Science, no. 57. (New York: Greenwood, 1986), p. 55.

50. Alley, "Staffing Technical Services," p. 482.

51. Martin, Murray. *Issues in Personnel Management in Academic Libraries*. (Greenwich, CT: JAI, 1986), p. 199.

52. Veaner, Allen B. "1985-1995: The Next Decade in Academic Librarianship, Part I," *College & Research Libraries* 46 (1985), p. 222.

53. Preston, "How Will Automation Affect Cataloging," p. 133.

54. Schumann, Patricia Glass. "Library Networks: A Means, Not an End," *Library Journal* 112 (1987):34.

55. Horny, "Fifteen Years of Automation," p. 74.

56. Intner, Sheila. "Debunking More Cataloging Myths," *Technicalities* 7 (April 1987):10.

57. Intner, "Debunking More Cataloging Myths," p. 10.

58. "The Catalogerless Society," *American Libraries* 14 (1983):730.

59. Martin, *Issues in Personnel Management*, p. 201.

60. De Gennaro, "Libraries & Networks in Transition," p. 1046.

61. Hafter, Ruth. "Born Again Cataloging in the Online Networks," *College & Research Libraries* 47 (1986):354.

62. Preston, "How Will Automation Affect Cataloging," p. 134.

63. Fenley, Judith G. and Sarah D. Irvine. "The Name Authority Co-Op (NACO) Project at the Library of Congress: Present and Future," *Cataloging & Classification Quarterly* 7 (Winter 1986):7-18.

64. Repp, Joan M. "The Response of the Cataloger and the Catalog to Automation in the Academic Library Setting," *Advances in Library and Administration and Organization* 5 (Greenwich, CT: JAI, 1986), p. 72.

65. Hafter, "Born Again Cataloging," p. 364.

66. Ms. Rather, in remarks delivered upon her receipt of the Margaret Mann Award, noted that her father had told her that a girl would do anything, so long as she didn't learn to type.

67. Atkinson, "Closing the Catalog," p. 129.

68. Horny, "Fifteen Years of Automation," p. 73.

69. Repp, "Response of the Cataloger," p. 81.

70. Martin, *Issues in Personnel Management*, p. 200.

71. Freedman, "Future of Technical Services," p. 1199.

72. "CCS Task Force on Education and Recruitment for Cataloging Report, June, 1986," *RTSD Newsletter* 11 (1986):73-74.

73. Auld, Lawrence W.S. "The King Report: New Directions in Library and Information Science Education. A Close Look at a Controversial Study," *College & Research Libraries News* 48 (1987):178.

74. "CCS Task Force on Education and Recruitment for Cataloging," p. 73.

75. Preston, "How Will Automation Affect Cataloging," p. 131.

76. Funk and Bishoff, "By Any Name," p. 591.

77. Oyler, "Education for Technical Services," p. 597.

78. Holley, "Future of Catalogers," p. 92.

79. Auld, "The King Report," p. 178.

80. Intner, Sheila. "A Giant Step Backwards for Technical Services," *Library Journal* 110 (1985):43-45.

81. Gorman, "On Doing Away with Technical Services," p. 435.

82. Intner, Sheila. "Debunking More Cataloging Myths," *Technicalities* 7 (April 1987):10.

83. Holley, "Future of Catalogers," p. 92.

84. Gorman, "Technical Services, 1984-2001," p. 70.

85. Alley, "Staffing Technical Services," p. 483.

Reshaping Technical Services for Effective Staff Utilization

Brian Alley

RECENT HISTORY

In a great many libraries, perhaps the majority, the ordering, cataloging and processing of materials has constituted, over the years, a labor-intensive activity operating under the title of technical services. Within that unit librarians, paraprofessionals, clerks, and students all engaged in activities that were fairly well defined in their job descriptions. There were lots of exceptions, but for the most part only the catalogers cataloged and other librarians did those things that only librarians were permitted to do, while the other levels of the technical services labor chain were equally limited and restricted in terms of their range of allowable activities. The productivity generated by these units was measured in terms of volumes cataloged or processed. Rarely in the reporting of accomplishments did the technical services librarians show the relationship between the mountains of unprocessed materials and the annual total of materials acquired.

MANAGING THE INFORMATION EXPLOSION

Nearly every large library from the late 1950s through the early 1970s carried a large backlog of unprocessed materials. There were good reasons for the backlogs. The libraries of the nation were buying books and materials at unprecedented rates and the technical services personnel were simply unprepared to deal with the volume. They simply couldn't gear up to meet the new demands for mass production for a variety of reasons, not the least of which was a general unwillingness to face the possible consequences of a major

Brian Alley is Dean of Library Services at Sangamon State University, Springfield, IL.

overhaul of the entire technical services process. In the late 1950s and early 1960s librarians were concerned with the information explosion and looking to mainframe computers as a means of storing and retrieving information. By today's standards this notion seems ludicrous for only with current CD-ROM technology do we even begin to get close to the kind of storage possibilities we were projecting then. Somehow we felt the punched card systems were a cost effective mechanism and were actually capable of changing the way libraries operated. Some punched card systems did indeed find their way into libraries but as circulation systems, not for the conversion of printed materials into computer databases.

Technical services technology of the period still revolved around the typewriter with librarians praising the IBM model D because it could be fitted with a script "L" and shunning the Selectric because it couldn't. The Xerox 914 made its debut in the early sixties and it, together with the models that followed, produced millions of poor quality catalog cards for the libraries of the nation. Throughout this period libraries were snatching up bits of technology here and there and attempting to piece together tools to cope with the heavy influx of materials. They were struggling to create the means to deal with the mass cataloging and processing of materials and drawing on the skills and talents of a generation of librarians who were still oriented to the 3 × 5 card. The odds and ends of technology that we were able to adapt to our needs presented us with some minor internal training needs but never really changed the personnel requirements for technical services work.

It wasn't until the early to mid 1970s that library oriented technology in the form of The Ohio College Library Center began to impact on libraries. Although it retained the 3 × 5 format it produced cataloging in a fraction of the time local libraries could generate it and at a cost they could afford. It was library technology created *by* librarians *for* librarians and it worked. Backlogs were reduced and a semblance of efficiency began to creep into technical services units that had until then been regarded as bottomless pits when it came to their funding requirements.

STAFFING PRACTICES CHANGE

The 1970s technology produced something else for technical services watchers. It changed the nature of the want ads and for a very few qualified applicants it provided an entree to a job interview they might not otherwise have gotten. Libraries weren't just looking for mere catalogers, they now wanted catalogers with OCLC experience. They wanted to hire people who had the technical skills to deal effectively with a whole new way to generate library cataloging. Ultimately, library schools began to instruct students in the mysteries of online cataloging and in the libraries, on-the-job training took care of the rest. Well, not all of the rest. A number of older librarians chose to avoid online cataloging in particular and automation in general until retirement.

The microcomputer of today met with easy acceptance in technical services possibly because librarians working with OCLC had gotten accustomed to green phosphor CRTs and multicolored keyboards and were not frightened by the microcomputer the way some of their colleagues had been by the first cataloging terminals. Also, their public service counterparts had been involved in database searching for some time so the notion of librarians using terminals wasn't altogether new. The microcomputer created yet another demand for people with OCLC and microcomputer skills.

It's a story of ever increasing acceptance and reliance on labor saving technology. Through it all we have focused on technology and have advertised for technical skills. We have really neglected to take a hard look at our human resources in terms of designing the kind of organizations that not only have the technical competence to keep pace with rapidly developing technology, but also the kinds of managers who understand systems, budgets, and the art of matching people to jobs.

The technology, if used properly, creates opportunities for change. So far, we have used the new technology to help us cope with production problems. It has earned an enviable track record and for the foreseeable future we will be confirmed technology advocates. But taking advantage of specialized technology is only part of the game if we are serious about libraries becoming the major information brokers in the 1990s and beyond.

If the technical services units are going to contribute effectively to the total library mission they need to address the cost of doing business. That brings us right back to the nature of our activities and how we spend our budgets. We are still very much a labor-intensive business. Even with all the automation, too many of us still staff our technical services units to the hilt and persist in carrying on a great many routines virtually unchanged from decades past.

Attempts to address the staffing issues haven't had much of an impact partly because it is difficult to impose sweeping changes on organizations in which tradition counts for so much. The people in the back rooms of libraries routinely handle the detailed work that requires painstakingly careful attention to what many of us would call minutiae. Replacing those routines with a new order isn't all that easy to accomplish. The advent of OCLC scared the daylights out of lots of librarians who internalized their trauma but nevertheless experienced it. For many of them, for years technical services was a safe island in a sea of change and then along came a Beehive terminal and threatened their very existence.

One barrier to efficient and cost-effective technical services is the continued use of professional librarians for a multitude of jobs that are dangerously close to being classified as clerical. A number of those jobs are in the area of cataloging. Professional catalogers were is great demand back in the 1960s. That demand continued into the 1970s and is still with us today. If you don't believe it you haven't been scanning the ads in *The Chronicle of Higher Education* lately.

OPTIONS

If controlling and even reducing the cost of human services in the technical services organization is ever going to become a reality, at least part of the process will have to involve completely rethinking the kinds of skill and experience requirements that make up a successful technical services operation. Can you envision a mere handful of librarians in the entire technical operation with only one of them a professional cataloger? If you can, then there are a few "ifs" for you to consider as we continue to develop the scenario.

If your library can accept shared cataloging and take it "as is" without modification, if you can operate your acquisition department strictly as a purchasing arm of your organization with trained order clerks, but without a professional librarian, you are ready to start making some savings. If you can catalog your collection using the bibliographic utility of your choice with a clerical staff, you've got substantial savings in store for you. If you can use such labor savers as approval plans, blanket orders, contract cataloging and processing, or central processing, you've got the potential for additional labor savings. These are just a few of the kinds of "ifs" that can produce real savings in the personnel budget of your technical services operation if you are willing to try some new strategies.

To produce really significant savings from technical services staff reorganization, the resulting organization must limit the use of professional librarians primarily to such areas as training, managing and supervision. Librarians are the highest paid members of our organizations. The more of them we hire, the greater the cost of doing business. When we hire librarians as trainers we hire experts who are utilizing their professional skills to their greatest extent. Nonprofessional staff can easily be trained to catalog and order materials and to perform any and all related tasks. They do exceptionally well with the technology that exists in libraries. With a trainer-in-residence available to provide continuous support and guidance, all things are possible. The position of trainer will require a generalist technical services librarian to serve as teacher/manager/coordinator.

In the very near future all types of libraries are going to have the option of ordering materials and seeing them arrive fully processed from the vendor. Processing in this instance includes all the little inhouse processing details and devices we spend millions on today: spine labels, bar codes, pockets, and security devices. An opportunity to remove these manual chores from the library is one more reason for considering a major change in the way we organize and staff our technical services operations.

WHERE ARE WE HEADED?

That all depends on how soon we recognize the need to revise our thinking about staffing technical services in the high tech phase of library development. The opportunities are there for enterprising library administrators who want to offer more services to their patrons. With the savings gained from a thoughtful, careful reorganization and reorientation of technical services, more professionals can be provided to support the public service operation. If providing the highest quality public service for the library community is part of the institutional mission, then shifting personnel dollars from a revitalized, reorganized, cost-effective technical services unit to public services makes good sense. The time to begin is now and the greater the effort, the bigger the rewards. Doing the technical services job the labor-intensive way is about to become a thing of the past. The end products will still have to be produced and library staff are definitely going to be involved, but not at the levels we required in the past—not unless we are determined to ignore the budget realities of the 1980s and the potential to make substantial cost savings for our libraries.

STARTING THE PROCESS

Starting the process will require considerable planning as well as plenty of thoughtful consideration of the people involved. If shaping new staffing patterns can be a group effort, so much the better. As a community effort with all of the technical services staff involved in the planning and an assurance that jobs are not at stake, the process can actually produce some enthusiastic supporters and proceed in an orderly, productive fashion.

Whether we start the process now or a year from now, reorganization for many of us will be inevitable. The opportunities are simply too obvious to resist. When it comes to deciding which libraries offer the best opportunities for technical services reorganization, academic libraries will probably present some of the most obvious cases. Public libraries have already had lots of experience with change and have made a number of modifications in technical services staffing patterns to make their organizations more effective and cost-efficient.

The benefits to be derived from reshaping the technical services staff to fit the needs of modern libraries are many. They have implications throughout the organization and the library. But they are especially important for the technical services personnel. They can look forward to a much more rewarding role for librarians and clerks alike. Each one can become more vital to the ultimate success of a leaner, meaner, and more cost-effective organization.

Educating Librarians and Support Staff for Technical Services

Gisela M. Webb

While all library functions have been affected by the use of automation during the last three decades, the technical service areas have benefitted and changed most. Cataloging has been revolutionized through the use of shared databases provided by bibliographic utilities, while the acquisition of materials has been standardized and streamlined through computerization. Although there may be a few librarians left who mourn the loss of the good old times, most have adapted well to current levels of computerization and are willing to acknowledge the freedom gained from the drudgeries of the past. Many even express a sense of pride in mastering the unanticipated technological changes which affected their work and careers so profoundly. *But* having found a state of relative equilibrium in technical services again, librarians and administrators are beginning to raise some uneasy questions.

- Where do libraries go from here?
- If this is only the beginning, will we be able to cope with future changes?
- Is there a place for current staff in these libraries of the future?
- What alternatives do we have if we decide that some of us can no longer practice our chosen profession?
- What can we do now to prepare ourselves for handling future expectations and/or create career alternatives?
- What kind of person do we need to hire now to help us bring about the library of the future?

Gisela M. Webb is Assistant Director of Libraries for Administrative Services at Texas Tech University, Lubbock, TX.

111

Paraprofessional and high level support staff, while relishing the opportunities to grow and assume more complex responsibilities, also show signs of unease. Proud of their expanded role within an automated library, they try to redefine their duties as librarians delegate more and more routine and supervisory responsibilities. They demand to be acknowledged as the backbone of library operations through higher status and compensation.

Since today's library staffs "are caught in the middle of the information revolution, between traditional . . . conservation and tantalizing possibilities of the high-tech world,"[1] library managers and leaders try to anticipate the future and provide the means of educating staff for as yet undefinable job responsibilities.

Where do we begin? According to Keith Cottam the "central issues are those of role, behavior, and adaptation to change in the information age,"[2] while Allen Veaner similarly "urges librarians to move away from a 'passive, reactive behavior' and adopt an active creative role, . . . for librarianship on the highest plane is primarily an intellectual enterprise involving ideas, knowledge, people, and communication systems."[3]

But how do we change people who have largely self selected into a profession they perceived as stable and comfortable, with a minimum of stress rather than a profession that would be destined to play a critical role in the emerging information age? Can we really give up our "file" orientation and our often unnecessarily complex procedures, which have provided us with power bases and a sense of importance, and what are we gaining in return?

THE EMERGING ROLE OF
THE PROFESSIONAL LIBRARIAN

As a result of automation, many responsibilities previously performed by professional librarians are now delegated to students, clerical, and paraprofessional employees. Librarians' work in turn will become more complex and sophisticated and will exhibit a service orientation rather than focusing on files and procedures. They will know "why and what to acquire and how to acquire it, . . . how to organize recorded knowledge; and . . . how to work as information access experts and service agents for library users."[4]

Professional librarians of the future will also play a more active role in the management and administration of their organization. They will be involved in analyzing the specific needs of the environment in which they function, develop appropriate missions and goals to meet those needs, and manage the human resources to implement the programs serving their constituents.

In order to do that effectively, librarians will generally be aware of trends not only in librarianship, but society at large, they will share their own thoughts, experiences, successes, and failures through professional activities, and they will continuously educate themselves to stay knowledgeable about technologies and other matters affecting their work. They will become specialists in library administration, budgets, personnel, public relations, fund-raising, and information technologies, besides refining their traditional professional skills of evaluating, organizing and delivering information. Continuing education, even certification, will become a must, an integral part of one's career development.

THE EMERGING ROLE OF SUPPORT STAFF

As librarians have and continue to assume the truly professional responsibilities of their positions, more of their duties are and will be delegated to high level support staff. "Support staff activities cover a wide range of essential work, including the tasks of inputting, coding, and verifying bibliographic data, maintaining book funds, ordering, claiming serials, filing, non-original cataloging, and other tasks that support the library's daily operations."[5] Although this downward shift of responsibilities creates more rewarding jobs and career growth for the usually abundant number of highly educated and motivated support staff members, it may also lead to growing frustration and dissatisfaction with their status and compensation.

Richard Dougherty alerted the profession about this mixed blessing ten years ago when he wrote that as librarians become more involved in the governance of libraries and spend more time at conferences, the tasks they performed will have to be delegated to assistants. While this process of reassignment creates new opportunities for library assistants, the added responsibilities are not necessarily accompanied by higher salaries. In many cases, highly skilled and eager paraprofessionals have exhibited more creativity and risk taking in assuming new responsibilities than professionals who have difficulties in letting go of comforting, but routine tasks. According to Barbara Conroy "paraprofessional have often been the first skilled library personnel in new areas such as outreach, audiovisual services, and automated circulation.''[6]

Although we can expect continuing positive responses from the highly educated and motivated support staff members to expanding responsibilities, library administrators must create true career ladders to reward their increasing technical and subject expertise. This will require continuous and often frustrating efforts to educate administrators of a library's parent organization about the emerging nature of the library profession itself and the crucial role the support staff plays in improving the services provided.

REQUIREMENTS FOR TECHNICAL SERVICES LIBRARIANS IN THE 21ST CENTURY

Analyzing current job advertisements for both professional and support staff positions, certain trends can be ascertained. Libraries appear to be seeking "total librarians," professionals who are flexible and want to work in more than one functional area, librarians who are willing to perform multiple roles, grouped around their subject expertise. Simultaneously, support staff without MLSs are hired to replace librarians in the areas of circulation, interlibrary loan, stack maintenance, copy and standard cataloging, and support services in acquisitions.

Current trends require that just at the time when the profession is experiencing recruitment problems, libraries are faced with the opportunity to carefully determine if an MLS is necessary or even desirable for all positions previously held by professionals. Keith Cottam advises that

> . . . in setting employee selection criteria, employers are well advised to respond with reason and common sense to the changing occupational and professional nature of librarianship, to comply with the letter as well as the spirit of legal constraints and regulatory guidelines, and to analyze job requirements carefully and deliberately in order to determine necessary qualifications for applicants.[7]

One implication of these trends for the education of technical services librarians is that managers who now make recruitment decisions need to be able to identify the truly professional responsibilities of positions under their authority. While this can be done routinely as professional vacancies occur, the more demanding task is to raise the awareness of the remaining professionals who find it comforting to continue to function at nonprofessional levels. Involving such reluctant librarians in the process of determining job requirements and selection criteria for vacant positions may be a first step to address this issue. Service on search committees can help such staff members to understand and articulate organizational expectations to fellow committee members and candidates. In addition, such service will require the evaluation of prospective staff members in terms of the new organizational and professional expectations.

As new colleagues start to function at higher levels, managers can help those unwilling to let go of clerical tasks by continuing to assign them to task forces and committees which address professional concerns. Because these new involvements will inevitably cause time constraints, reluctant professionals may be more willing to identify those duties which can be transferred to lower level staff to ease their own frustrations. As good management practices like annual goal setting, evaluations, and merit increases become integral parts of library administration, increased involvement in overall library concerns can be encouraged and reinforced regularly, formalized through committee assignments, and rewarded as appropriate.

The creation of bridge positions presents other opportunities to foster a better understanding of a library's mission and goals by technical services librarians. Working in more than one functional area means reporting to more than one person usually with different managerial styles and different perceptions and priorities. Adjusting to these differences means reconstructing ones own philosophy, an often painful yet broadening experience. Involvement in collection development, bibliographic instruction, or reference service, for example, not only educates technical services professionals about the actual impact of their work on the library users, but continuously requires them to articulate logical and polite responses to questions challenging the validity or even necessity of their work. The need for accountability does not have to be explained very often when technical services librarians are asked to justify their professional decisions not only to their peers, but to library users.

Not all technical services librarians will be responsive to these changes. Many are not interested in library wide concerns and have chosen a career in cataloging or acquisitions because it met their needs for predictability, structure, and setting their own work pace and priorities. Some will be close enough to retirement, that their lifelong contribution to the institution must be weighted against the need to implement changes. A postponement of new directions may be advisable for a short time period or, if this is not possible, early retirement may be suggested as an option to preserve the dignity of long-term employees who are threatened and/or confused by the demands of technology or participative management styles. Others, too young to retire, yet unable to change, may need to be transferred to more narrowly focused positions, or in more extreme cases, terminated.

Educating professionals for the opportunities of the future is a responsibility which must be shared by the individual librarian and the library. Well defined in-house staff development programs can help prepare professionals for their new roles and provide them with some of the skills necessary to perform increasingly complex duties. Deliberations leading to organizational change and planning for implementing new technologies should ideally include staff development and training programs.

While training for new automated systems is often carefully designed by vendors and library automation staff, many libraries are simultaneously experimenting with programs on how to educate staff to cope with the stress of changing workflow, work relationships, and management styles. Staff development programs which teach new communications patterns, management and supervisory skills, which explain the nature of change and its implications for library organizations and their staffs, which demonstrate how well managed organizations function, and which teach constructive interpersonal relations skills can create an organizational climate where the introduction of new automated systems is eagerly anticipated. Staff will have the skill to anticipate problems and address them with confidence.

"For in-depth specialty skills, personnel will probably continue to rely on outside continuing education sources, such as that from associations and education institutions. From these, they return to apply their learning in their unique library circumstances."[8] Although institutions can support these activities through travel funds and time, librarians themselves will need the initiative and desire to pursue their specialties and be professionally active. The benefits of such activities transcend the enhancement of specialty skills, by providing opportunities to practice leadership skills in association committees, to build a professional network which may be helpful in career advancement, and to create an awareness of professional trends and issues of the future. These intangible benefits will prepare professionals to be proactive rather than reactive in the change process which librarians will experience in the next two decades and beyond.

Other continuing learning opportunities are often provided by library schools and library experts within a state or region, who are willing to educate through workshops, conferences, on-site visits to institutions, or internships.

REQUIREMENTS FOR SUPPORT STAFF

As the role of support staff members in academic libraries increases, administrators need to find ways to develop, recognize, and reward the human resources which will become largely responsible for the day to day library operations. To do their jobs well, paraprofessionals will need to be educated about the interrelationships of their work with the responsibilities of other departments. Their goals must be broadened to include the understanding that their expanded responsibilities will free professionals to plan for and pursue the mission of the entire library and the profession.

Managers who are cognizant of the important role paraprofessionals are assuming, already maximize their input in library issues. Modelled on the increased involvement of professionals in library governance, paraprofessionals should be included in all deliberations and decisions concerning their departmental affairs. This can take the form of participation in analyzing staffing needs, service on search committees for professional and nonprofessional positions, the development of training plans for new staff members and cross-training opportunities for existing staff, and the inclusion on task forces and committees. Since support staff members in many cases will be more knowledgeable about work flow than the professional in charge of a department, it is logical that their input needs to be considered before changes or technological innovations are introduced. This involvement will ensure that details are not overlooked and enhance cooperation during implementation phases.

Libraries around the country are adding new specialty position and new classification to recognize and compensate paraprofessionals for their increased expertise and contribution. Clear distinctions between primarily clerical positions and paraprofessional positions with broad decision making responsibilities are emerging. Implications are that clerical personnel can no longer hope to progress automatically into higher support staff positions, based on longevity and experience alone. Library managers will need to clarify these newly emerging requirements for career advancement. In many instances additional education will be necessary for clerical staff if they want to be considered for specialty or paraprofessional positions. They will have to demonstrate their ability to deal with the complexities of ever changing work demands and their willingness to continually upgrade their skills. These newly created positions will also set some paraprofessionals apart from other support staff members in lower classifications. Most often, supervisory responsibilities are shifted from librarians to the high level support staff members, who need time to adjust to their new roles. Managers need to be aware of the stresses created by new work relationships. While some paraprofessionals will assume their new responsibilities with ease, others will feel unable to become supervisors of peers or friends.

Libraries may offer departmental and crossdepartmental training programs to provide learning opportunities for upwardly mobile clerks and broaden their perspectives of library work. If successful, clerical staff will understand the organizational need for highly educated and motivated individuals in the complex positions of paraprofessionals. Managers interested in developing their staff must strive to be role models and encourage continuing education efforts. They need to point out that self-improvement prepares individuals not only for positions with more responsibility, but also for coping with changes in society as a whole.

Administrators will find, as in the professional ranks, support staff members who are unwilling or unable to accept the new expectations and requirements. Here too, goal-setting sessions, evaluations, increased feedback, and grievances can be used to clarify issues and educate staff. Those unwilling to let go of outdated expectations will likely end up leaving the organization. A higher turnover rate in support staff positions may develop during this transitional period but will also increase the momentum to imbue support staff members with a new organizational philosophy and new values.

A higher turnover rate will also make it necessary to develop standardized, comprehensive training programs to ensure continuing operations when staff members leave. These programs can include formalized orientations and training plans, procedures manuals, hands-on exercises, and groups discussions to name a few. Barbara Conroy points out that

> in-house staff development can make good use of technology to use, and perhaps, to produce, packaged learning modules particularly valuable for orientation and learning reinforcement. Audiotapes, videotapes, microfiche and computer assisted instruction may be produced in-house, purchased from outside, or developed collaboratively through libraries having similar needs. With these means general orientation to a unit or a piece of equipment, or instructions for procedures or processes, are possible and conducted with endless patience and consistency. Such packages enable staff members to become self-instructional learners. At the same time, they demystify the technology and provide freedom to schedule learning to fit an individual's needs.[9]

The acquisition of integrated automated systems by libraries has also hastened their need to formalize initial and continuing training programs. The pioneers stress the importance of preparing and training staff before a system actually is installed. Pre-installation training should familiarize staff with the basic components of the chosen system and how it will likely affect departmental and library operations. Implications for individual jobs can be discussed and staff members can mentally prepare for taking on changed responsibilities. Pre-implementation training also can prepare staff for difficulties which inevitably arise with such drastic changes, and teach individuals how to cope with the frustrations of malfunctions, initially slower work flow, decreased or increased levels of decision-making, and changed work environments.

Once a system is installed, consideration must be given to who needs to be trained first, how many people can be trained at one time, what is the right amount of hands-on experience, how much can people absorb at one time, who will best conduct training sessions and who will evaluate their effectiveness. Needed above all are open and constructive communication patterns, involvement in decision-making, and flexibility within a supportive organizational climate.

CONCLUSIONS

The library profession is entering a new era. Anticipation of and anxiety about the future permeate library organizations and professional meetings. While some brave souls try to predict the specific implications the information age will have for our institutions and careers, for most of us the future is difficult to conceptualize. But we all agree that we are entering perhaps the most significant period in the development of our profession and that we must actively participate in the shaping of our future. How can we do that? By examining the past and letting go of unnecessary assumptions, traditions, procedures, by experimenting with automation and management practices, by taking risks, by thinking globally and holistically, by creating opportunities for ourselves and providing them for colleagues and staff, by being accountable and ethical.

Educating technical services librarians and support staff for the future will mean instilling new visions and values, setting a good example, and encouraging each person to become the best clerk, the best paraprofessional, the best librarians they can be. This will require the efforts and cooperation of all and will prepare libraries to play the significant role they deserve in a more civilized world.

NOTES

1. Barbara B. Moran, *Academic Libraries: The Changing Knowledge Center of Colleges and Universities* (ASHE-ERIC Higher Education Research Reports, No. 8), Washington: Association for the Study of Higher Education, 1984, p. xiii.

2. Keith M. Cottam, "The MLS: For the Public Good or Our Own Good?" *Library Journal* 111 (February 15, 1986): 112.

3. Cottam, p. 113.

4. Cottam, p. 113.

5. Moran, p. 43.

6. Barbara Conroy, "The Human Element: Staff Development in the Electronic Library," *Drexel Library Quarterly* 17 (Fall 1981): 91.

7. Keith M. Cottam, *ALA, the MLS and Professional Employment* (American Library Association Council Document # 10), Washington: American Library Association, 1984, p. 2.

9. Conroy, p. 102.

10. Conroy, p. 102.

Impact of Automation
on Technical Services

Dana C. Rooks
Linda L. Thompson

The technical process aspects of libraries—cataloging, circulation, acquisitions, and serials control—were the first, and most logical operations, to be automated. Technical services processing in libraries traditionally has been a costly labor-intensive operation, beset with backlogs of work and overburdened with redundancies. A primary goal of library technical services automation—from the beginnings of OCLC to the fully integrated library systems of today's libraries—has been to increase productivity, broaden accessibility of information, eliminate duplication of effort and ultimately, to enhance service to the library's clientele. Much of this has been accomplished.

Automation of library technical services has been occurring at a very rapid pace. Changes have been so fast and so sweeping, that the true impact of automation on technical services has yet to be adequately evaluated. In too many instances, libraries have found that the technology is in control of the human being rather than the human being directing the use of the technology.

The need to fully analyze and evaluate the impact of automation on technical services is long overdue. Library managers can no longer afford to limit their attention to the technical aspects of hardware, software, and telecommunications issues. The impact on human resources and the organization must be given equal, if not greater, time and attention. If library automation is ever to achieve its full potential and measure up to the ambitious long-range goals and expectations by which most automation projects are justified,

---

Dana C. Rooks is Assistant Director for Administration, and Linda L. Thompson is Assistant Director for Bibliographic Services at the University of Houston Libraries, Houston, TX.

there must be a successful resolution of the accompanying organizational and personnel conflicts and concerns.

This article addresses the impact of automation on technical services in four key areas—job-related concerns, the organizational structure, recruitment and training, and ergonomic issues. While there are no simple solutions or ready answers, this article attempts to raise some of the issues, point out areas of potential conflict or concern, and offer the beginnings of possible solutions.

JOB-RELATED CONSIDERATIONS

Computer technology and the conversion of manual systems and processes to computerized systems is a reality which permeate our daily lives. From the convenience of unstaffed automated teller machines to the speed and accuracy of optical scanners at the grocery check-out counter, the computerization of work is an ever expanding phenomenon. With this increased emphasis on technology comes the harsh reality of job loss, obsolescence of skills, and decreased opportunities. The fears and anxieties which accompany automation in the workplace are real and their impact on library technical services staff is only beginning to be recognized and understood. Indeed, one of the most significant impacts of automation on technical services has been the direct effect on technical services staff and their jobs. Managers in libraries which are implementing automation in their technical service operations must be aware of the many job-related issues which will concern their employees and be prepared to address these concerns openly and honestly.

The first and foremost issue to be addressed is which jobs will be affected and what plans exist to deal with the elimination of current jobs and the creation of new jobs. Some of the questions to be resolved are:

- Will the number of jobs required in the automated system equal the number existing in the current system?
- Will all current staff be retained?
- Will all current staff be offered the opportunity for retraining?
- Will the skills and abilities of current staff be compatible with the skills required for the new system?
- What options are available for lay-offs or redeployment under existing collective bargaining agreements or other institutional policies and commitments?

Fears related to job loss, obsolescence of skills, and even loss of status are a natural occurrence among staff when automation is introduced. For example, staff who file in the card catalog will soon realize that their current task will be eliminated with the introduction of the online catalog. However, the newly created need for database maintenance of the online catalog records may not be so readily apparent to these employees. There is a strong relationship between these two tasks, and retraining of current card catalog filing staff to handle database maintenance responsibilities is a logical progression.

However, while the apparent solution in this example may be a redeployment of staff from card filing to database maintenance, even this answer is incomplete because of the disparity in the number of staff required in the two operations. As expected, automation significantly increases the efficiency of maintaining a catalog. In a card catalog, each new title requires the alphabetizing and filing of multiple cards. To revise or withdraw a record requires that each of these multiple cards be located individually and revised or removed. In an online catalog a new record is input once and the machine handles the indexing and recording of all entries regardless of the number. Similarly, to revise or delete a record requires only one step to identify and alter or delete any record. The need to physically move from one cabinet to another as the individual locates multiple cards, possibly in duplicate catalogs, is eliminated. Therefore, the process of entering, revising, and withdrawing records in an online system requires only a portion of the staff necessary for the same tasks in a manual card system.

As a result of the increased productivity from automation, the organization is left with the question of how or if to utilize the remaining staff. One natural option is to allocate the "excess" staff to expand services or to do those jobs which could never be completed because of inadequate staffing—clearing backlogs, cleaning up the bibliographic database, cataloging material such as government documents, maps, or manuscripts which are uncataloged.

Utilizing excess staff to expand current services is an ideal, but frequently not a feasible, alternative given the budgetary constraints of many libraries. While staff reductions become possible in some areas, automation simultaneously generates the need for new skills and new positions which did not exist previously. Often, these new functions require a high level of skill which may not exist among current staff members in the present technical services operation.

For example, some of the typical functions in a manual versus automated technical services department might be as follows:

Technical Services Functions

Traditional	Automated
Card Preparation	Database Maintenance
Card Filer	Data Entry Operator
Bookkeeper	Systems Operator
Clerk Typist	Systems Programmer
Acquisitions Order Clerk	Systems Analyst
Serials Check-In Clerk	
Serials Claiming Clerk	
Authority Clerk	

Many of the functions handled by staff members within the traditional technical services operations may be handled independently by the computer, with only limited intervention by a staff member — for example, authority control. The computer will verify the correct entry through the authority control index and only report problem entries for handling by staff. In other operations, fewer staff will be required to complete the same function in an automated system, because of the greater efficiencies in computerized systems. For example, automated serial check-in eliminates the need to sort or alphabetize issues before check-in since issues can be checked in any order through any of multiple terminals regardless of the access point. There is no need to coordinate work among the various sections of the central serials record files.

However, just as the system reduces or eliminates the need for some functions, it also creates the need for jobs which did not exist in the previous operation. These may include systems operators, programmers, and analysts. Each of these jobs require highly-developed skills and training which may prohibit the direct transfer of staff from obsolete or extraneous tasks. It is also unlikely that lower-level clerk typists and card filers can feasibly be retrained to assume these responsibilities. Therefore, unless a library can afford the cost of these new positions, the funding for additional positions must be generated through the elimination of excess and obsolete positions.

Typically this conversion of positions can be accomplished through normal attrition as the system is phased in. The transition from manual to automated routines is a gradual process. Not all new positions will be needed immediately, nor can all manual functions be eliminated simultaneously. Therefore, if the library has developed a careful plan for the transition, it is quite possible that attrition will eliminate the need for future layoffs.

In addition to concerns over the impact of technology on the number of jobs, technical services staff will be concerned about their place within the organization. These concerns will focus on questions such as:

— Will my value to the organization increase?
— Will my current job classification be changed?
— How will automation impact opportunities for promotion and advancement?

It is an indisputable fact that automation will and must change employee work patterns. The application of technology to technical processes not only leads to major productivity increases, but also to significant changes in the parameters and definitions of existing jobs. As evidenced above, staff will be confronted with an entirely new series of job titles with totally or partially changed job content. In most organizations, this will mandate review and reclassification of many of these positions. Again this is a very frightening prospect to many employees, which they may perceive as a threat to their security.

Many employees will feel that their value to the organization is diminished within an automated system. In a manual system, information which is needed by many may be contained in a proprietary file accessible to one individual, thereby bestowing a unique sense of value and status to that individual. In an automated system, access to information is decentralized and readily accessible from remote terminals with no dependence upon a specific individual. For example, the status of an on order title can be easily and quickly checked from any terminal with access to the acquisitions system. Technology eliminates the need to request order information only from the staff member who maintains the order file. The information effectively becomes public information available at all times, regardless of who's on vacation, on a coffee break, or busy with other duties. Thus employees who were "keepers of information" in the paper dependent system may feel they are no longer of importance and they experience a sense of loss of value within the organization. If library managers are unaware of this effect and thus take no action to reestablish this loss of self-esteem, the result may be the loss of many highly-trained, skilled, and valuable employees.

A primary means of combatting the loss of self-worth is job enrichment. Technology will provide the opportunity to reevaluate and redesign many functions within technical services. How the organization restructures the functions of the automated system into new jobs is a key component of the success of the technology and its effect on retention of staff, motivation, and productivity in the future. Technology generates many routine and boring tasks, but it also creates challenging opportunities to expand and enrich jobs. Technical services managers must design the new jobs in a way that incorporates some of the challenging aspects along with the mundane routines, provides varied tasks, and allows a sense of self-worth if they are to attract and retain high quality staff. No job should be structured so that a staff member is tied to a terminal all day repeatedly performing a single function. This causes boredom and fatigue and may result in a decrease of productivity below the level prior to automating the process.

The decentralization of information in the automated system allows the organization to distribute tasks also. For example, serials staff might divide their time between check-in, claiming, and invoicing activities, rather than being assigned to a single function required by the location of information in a manual system. This diversity is more feasible in an automated system because the checking or error function of the technology and the compatibility of the various tasks within the systems have reduced the need for as much specialization. Therefore staff can be trained to perform a wider variety of tasks in an automated environment, as opposed to the manual systems. This will provide enrichment and decrease boredom which will result in greater motivation, self-esteem, and productivity.

Well-designed work assignments for staff working with machines can go far in providing a harmonious work environment and consequently, a successful integration of machines into the workplace. With careful planning, and a little innovation and creativity, the opportunity for effective job design to adapt to the technological changes can be a strong positive influence on the library for many years to come.

The restructuring of technical services as a result of automation additionally creates employee concerns in the area of relationships. These concerns will focus on such questions as:

— Will I be working with the same group of people?
— Who will be my supervisor?
— Will technical services become an assembly line operation?

Automation is dehumanizing to many people. Person-to-person interaction is replaced with human-to-machine interface. Instead of two staff members talking directly to each other, they will communicate via their computers which communicate with other computers. Socialization is reduced, mobility is minimized, and work groups are dispersed.

Employees who work in an environment which is machine-dependent develop a strong need to interact with other people. Supervisors must be sensitive to this need and provide opportunities for human interaction within the framework of the job. One such opportunity might involve formal or informal means for employees to share job-related information which leads to resolution of on-the-job problems.

The implementation of technology within a technical services operation can yield tremendous benefits for staff if adequate attention is devoted to the job-related aspects of automation. The primary focus should be how the system can be used to promote a more effective future for the library and its employees. Despite the dramatic changes which automation brings, it will still be people who determine the success of the organization.

ORGANIZATIONAL IMPLICATIONS

In a technical services operation with an automated, integrated or linked system, two factors are emerging that have the potential to have a profound impact on the organization. These two factors are: (1) the amount of control over the work provided by the automated system; and (2) the centralization of bibliographic and related information into one common file (regardless of whether this is an actual or virtual file) with distributed access throughout technical services. Both of these conditions will have an effect on the organizational structure, the workflow, and the manner in which technical services tasks are performed.

The first element, control over the work, changes the manner in which tasks are supervised or reviewed and the amount of decision-making required of staff for routine activities. An automated system is able to provide a variety of built-in mechanisms that check for errors and control consistency of data input. These mechanisms eliminate the need for much of the routine revision formerly provided by supervisors. For example, bibliographic records entering an online database are compared against system tables to ensure that the records meet the criteria established for a correctly formatted MARC record. The system determines if the required tags are present and whether the fixed fields have been coded properly. Since this level of revision is provided by the system, it is not necessary to devote staff time to this function. If the system finds an error, it will be indicated on an error or exception report. Usually the system will identify the specific error thus making it unnecessary to check the record for all possible errors. The fact that the staff member's attention is immediately focused on specifics makes it possible for lower level staff to correct these errors by referring to appropriate manuals.

Additionally, the capability of an automated system to provide control eliminates many routine and repetitive tasks such as checking headings in an authority file. A system with online authority control will maintain consistency of the headings used in the database with little human intervention. Those headings not found in the automated authority file by the system will appear on a report, and only these headings will require checking by a staff member.

As it becomes possible to automate more steps of an operation, even less decision-making will be required for routine nonproblematic situations. For example, consider the extent to which automation could be applied to serials check-in and the consequent increase in system control over the operation. A barcode has been developed by the Serials Industry Systems Advisory Committee (commonly referred to as the SISAC barcode) which supplies in machine-readable form the ISSN followed by issue specific information (comprised of date and volume/issue numbers). If three conditions are met, the item can be immediately and automatically checked-in with *no* human intervention other than the physical act of scanning the barcode: the SISAC barcode appears on the item, the terminal used for check-in has an optical or laser scanning device, and the system software is able to interpret and record the information contained in the SISAC barcode. The benefits of such an application are readily apparent; the task can be accomplished more efficiently, more accurately, and more economically.

While this last example of an automated application admittedly is not yet generally available, it does illustrate one of the ultimate goals of automating technical services operations: to minimize the amount of decision-making necessary to perform routine functions. The achievement of this goal would allow the largest part of the work load to be handled by relatively low level staff with very little task supervision required. Managers would then be free to focus on the problems and exceptions that occur, as well as to engage in other activities such as long-range planning.

The second element fostered by the implementation of linked or integrated systems, the centralization of information into one shared file, will change among other things, the way in which technical services staff view themselves and their work. An integrated auto-mated workflow is based on one common file — the bibliographic database — which is used by everyone. This file of bibliographic records will have other information linked to its records as neces-sary — order information, payment history, claiming records, circu-lation status, etc. But the same record, with the same bibliographic information, is the basis of the file and of each transaction that takes place.

The sharing of a common file will have a profound impact on the organization of technical services. In the past (and continuing into the present) so many technical services functions have revolved around the creation and maintenance (even protection) of localized or unique files, e.g., the on order file, the authority file, the shelf list, the serials check-in file, the binding file, etc. This contributed to an attitude of territoriality in technical services, not just vis-à-vis public services, but also among the various technical services units. Traditionally, most technical services staff have seen their jobs as very isolated from what others are doing, and so often their tasks have centered on creating specific types of records for a particular file. It was commonly acknowledged that these files contained in-formation which was both unique and redundant, yet before the advent of integrated automated systems there was no effective way to share the information and thus eliminate redundancy.

Sometimes this abundance of files has contributed to jobs in the workflow. For example, in some libraries when an item that is thought to be part of a series is ordered, the item (or the order, depending upon the organization of the workflow) is sent to another unit responsible for various authority files to have the series infor-mation verified. After this workflow deviation, the item continues on its process through technical services. In an automated workflow based on a shared file of bibliographic and processing information, series authority information would be readily available to the person receiving the item (or placing the order). In fact, in many instances the series information could be verified automatically by an online authority file. Another example of workflow deviation concerns those cataloging operations in which call numbers are checked against the shelf list (in order to catch duplicate call numbers or inappropriate assignment of call numbers) before the item is cataloged. With an automated system, the terminal operator will be able to check the call number online immediately prior to cataloging, or the system itself will compare the call number to those already in the call number index and then report possible problems via an online message or an error report, depending upon how records are being entered.

The centralization of bibliographic and other information into a common file of records that reflects each step of the workflow has the potential to break down the barriers that have existed between different work units. Technical services staff are realizing that they all need access to the same information, and that indeed their overall objectives are the same. Because the entire workflow depends upon the bibliographic record, it is important to obtain the most complete and accurate information as early in the process as possible, preferably when the order is placed.

As technical services activities become more automated and we begin to understand better the implications of automation, more logical and straightforward workflows will appear, and the organization will reflect and support that workflow. Communication will be more direct and less convoluted because the organization will be structured more logically and efficiently. Communication also will be enhanced because it will be based on common information in a shared file, rather than on a multitude of separate files. The records will become visible to the public earlier (e.g., on order information) and various transactions will be more readily available to both public and staff users (e.g., circulation status, etc.). As a result of these factors, staff will develop a greater appreciation for the contributions of their coworkers and the increased perception that everyone is working toward the same end: making information available to the users.

With the implementation of an integrated system, the workflow in technical services can be analyzed very effectively to determine that tasks are being performed in the most logical and efficient order. Automation dictates the development of a more logical workflow as an inherent part of the system and provides a variety of mechanisms by which this can be achieved. The two primary mechanisms are those mentioned above: system control and distributed access to information. Technical Services continues to have the same objectives, i.e., acquiring needed materials and making these materials accessible to the users in a timely fashion. The workflow of technical services will be based on function; however, an automated system will allow these functions to be organized and performed in a different order and manner.

As a result of these changes, the organizational structure of technical services will be based on the most logical automated workflow. Such a technical services might be comprised of the following:

- a unit for ordering, receiving, and editing—this group would be responsible for obtaining the correct bibliographic items *and* records;
- an original cataloging unit for those items for which records could not be found in any of the utilities of commercial sources;
- a continuations unit responsible for receipt of serials, added volumes, etc.;
- a marking and preservation group responsible for physical processing of materials, for preparing materials for the bindery, and for in-house binding and repair;
- a financial unit responsible for the payment of all invoices and the monitoring of funds and balances;
- and a database maintenance group that monitors error reports on the bibliographic and authority information in the system and performs corrections as necessary.

While this is one logical arrangement, obviously any organizational structure would have to be tailored to fit the local system and staff. Clearly, however, these three traditional departments of acquisitions, serials, and cataloging are no longer the only way or even the best way to organize technical services activities.

Automation will enable technical services staff to increase the accuracy and timeliness of their work output as well as the scope of the information provided. Most technical services operations will continue to be labor intensive, but the staff will be redistributed with fewer staff performing routine functions, such as check in of periodicals, and more staff being devoted to enhancing the level of service and amount of information provided, such as maintaining order status reports online and linked to the appropriate record. This activity would enable the public, as well as other staff members, to realize that the reason the library has not received the latest issue of a periodical title is because the publisher has fallen behind schedule, or that a requested item has not yet been published. The effective utilization of an automated system will permit routine tasks to be accomplished in a more efficient manner and human resources to be reallocated to activities that will enhance the level of service provided by the library as a whole.

In a fully automated technical services operation the staff will be able to do more and to do it better. This increased productivity and service will be provided by the same number of staff as employed at present (or perhaps even fewer). An integrated or linked system has the capacity to change how and where tasks are accomplished, thereby providing an opportunity to rethink the technical services workflow completely. Our goal when implementing these systems should be to use this opportunity to create a more efficient and effective technical services organization. As previously discussed, system control and distributed access to information are the two characteristics of such system that will have the greatest influence on the realization of this goal.

RECRUITMENT AND TRAINING ISSUES

An additional impact of automation on technical services is the increased significance of recruitment and training activities. Automation raises a number of questions regarding future needs and demands for staffing and training.

- What kind of qualifications will be needed by staff in the automated system?
- How can the organization best use its existing people?
- What extra skills will be required by the new system?
- What training will be needed to meet these skill requirements?
- Who will need training?
- What type of training is available and from whom?

Even the most experienced employees may approach change in the form of automation with some trepidation. Some will be afraid that they won't be able to learn the new techniques or that they won't be viewed as being equally competent in the new system. Fear of the unknown and of uncertainty is natural and the computer is a complex machine which embodies both aspects to many people. Also, technology-based systems are perceived to be more complex than manual ones which most people are used to and this overwhelms them and brings about anxieties in many staff. Often, people do not like change of any kind, and want their work environment to remain unchanged forever. Employees need reassurance that training will be provided and that they are capable of mastering the system.

An additional training need that is frequently overlooked is the need for supervisory training. Often the organization is so concerned with training the staff who operate the system that supervisors are ignored or given cursory training. Supervisors need to receive thorough training in the use of the system and the equipment. In some cases, the organizational changes which accompany automation will also create new supervisory positions. This creates the need for training these individuals in basic supervisory skills as well as systems training.

Planning and documentation of new procedures is mandatory for initial and continuing training efforts. Documentation can provide a means of quality control, consistency of operation, and a refresher or review for current staff as well as a primary training tool for new staff. The documentation must be kept current, however. As new releases of software are received or as procedures are adapted to organizational changes, these must be reflected in the documentation.

Training cannot end with the implementation and initial training period for systems operation. Automated systems are constantly being changed through updates, new applications, and revised procedures. These must be communicated systematically to staff through formal means such as update sessions, and informal methods such as supervisory monitoring and on-the-job training. Specific individuals should be identified as trainers and these responsibilities included in their duties. They should be given training in how to train and charged with both new employee training and continuing training for current staff. This will assist in providing quality and consistency in training programs and ensure that such activities will not fall by the wayside in the press of other activities.

Job descriptions for all current staff should be reviewed and revised to reflect changes in duties and responsibilities. Qualifications need to be carefully evaluated in light of the new responsibilities, and grade level reclassifications granted as warranted. This will prevent legal problems as well as aid in morale and motivation among staff.

Recruitment and training issues take on a new urgency with the implementation of automation. Well planned and implemented training programs can serve to allay fears and anxieties of staff, provide an opportunity to expand current skills, and ensure a smooth and successful transition to the new system.

ERGONOMIC CONSIDERATIONS

With the advent of automation, the physical appearance of technical services has changed. Devices such as terminals, printers, and cables have proliferated. While this article will not discuss ergonomics in any exhaustive sense, some key points need to be mentioned. Ergonomics can be defined simply as the technology of work design: the focus of ergonomics is upon the tasks that humans perform and how the workplace and the equipment help or impede those tasks.

The primary reason for applying ergonomic concepts to the workplace is to enhance productivity. Productivity will be improved if both physical and mental fatigue are reduced and if staff morale is good. Ergonomics can have an impact on all of these areas. If a terminal operator spends hours in an uncomfortable position because the work surface is the wrong height or the chair does not provide proper support, then both the quality and quantity of that person's work will be affected. Similarly, if there is a glare on the CRT screen, the consequent eye strain, and perhaps headache, will impact negatively on productivity.

Some of the factors to be considered when designing an automated work space are as follows:

1. Dimensions of the work table
   Will the keyboard be at the appropriate height to reduce strain on the wrists and forearms?
   Is the work surface large enough to accommodate printouts, books, or whatever will be needed at the computer terminal?

2. Chair design
   Is the seat height adjustable to accommodate different size people?
   Is the pressure and angle of the back adjustable so that proper support for the back is provided?
   Is the base of the chair balanced (usually this means five casters instead of four) so that it cannot be tipped over easily?
3. Height and angle of the CRT screen
   Are these adjustable so that different height people can use it without straining their neck and shoulders?
4. Placement of the terminals
   Is glare minimized with regard to sources of artificial and natural lighting?
   Are noise and other disruptions to concentration reduced in regard to traffic patterns?

Even this incomplete list of factors to consider indicates that thought should be given to how the equipment is to be used, who is going to use it, where it is to be used, and what else takes place in the immediate vicinity.

The above mentioned considerations will help to reduce mental fatigue as well as physical fatigue. Additionally, frequent breaks should be taken (at least every two hours) during work at the CRT, and if at all possible, the types of tasks done at the terminal should be alternated throughout an individual's schedule. Adhering to these guidelines will help to eliminate some of the tedium which can be inherent in these tasks, and which contributes to feelings of fatigue and boredom.

Attention to ergonomic factors when planning the work space and job design will improve staff morale. Partly this improvement can be attributed to the attention given to staff and how they perform their work. But also the work environment will be better and more conducive to working efficiently. These improvements in the workplace communicate to staff that they and the work they do are important.

Ergonomics, as it relates to technical services automation, involves a wide variety of factors, yet the two key objectives in creating a positive, ergonomic environment are reduction of physical and mental fatigue, and improvement of staff morale. These considerations should not be overlooked when introducing automated systems: they can have a direct impact on the staff's acceptance of the system which, in turn, will have an effect on the ultimate success or failure of the system implementation.

CONCLUSION

The greatest impact of technology on technical services has been change. Desks and book trucks are now interspersed among burgeoning numbers of terminals and printers. The traditional divisions of cataloging, acquisitions, and serials are far less distinct as automation dramatically alters the flow of material through the stages of processing. The machine performs many of the functions previously assigned to staff members. For example, the need for bookkeepers and card filers has disappeared, and instead technical services managers find they must hire, train, and supervise computer programmers and operators.

While automation has affected the very nature of library technical services, the overall goals remain the same today—the processing of library materials in a cost-effective and efficient manner while maintaining a high level of quality. Technology has only provided technical services staff with yet another tool in achieving this goal.

Notable Literature of the 1980s for Technical Services

Gloriana St. Clair
Jane Treadwell
Vicki Baker

The scope of this selected list includes articles in the management of technical services during the period from 1980 to the present. Selected articles have been used to indicate whole ranges of materials available to the tech services librarian seeking guidance from the literature. Collection development, the triggering mechanism for much technical services effort, is not within the purview of this piece, except as it relates to relations with vendors. Further, because the emphasis here has been on management issues, fine technical articles have also been passed over. Automation, education, managing external constituents, management techniques, personnel, and the role of tech services in the library are major divisions.

AUTOMATION

Atkinson, Hugh C. "The Impact of New Technology on Library Organization." *The Bowker Annual of Library & Book Trade Information*, 29th ed. New York: Bowker, 1984: 109-114.

Atkinson surveys the changes that automation has wrought in library organization, particularly in the cataloging and reference departments. He argues that the difference between original and rapid cataloging units is an attitudinal one, with workflow and organizational patterns changing as a result. In the future, he sees the catalog

Gloriana St. Clair is Assistant Director for Technical Services, Automation, and Administration at Oregon State University, Corvallis, OR. Jane Treadwell is Head of the Resource Development Division, and Vicki Baker is Original Cataloger for special format materials at Texas A&M University, College Station, TX.

facilitating decentralization of library functions, eventually including cataloging. Decentralization will call for a new type of library administrator, similar to the collection development officer in large academic libraries. These administrators will not so much supervise personnel but will provide "the intellectual administration of the function."

Bustion, Marifran, Jacque Halverson, and Laura Salas-Tull. "Serials Control Systems: An Annotated Bibliography." *Library High Tech Bibliography* (1987): 123-129.

Serials control systems will certainly continue to be an issue through the next decade. The authors wisely caution that systems described in their article may have become unavailable as the librarians read the article. The fifty-four articles briefed in the bibliography provide an overview of the state of serials automation in libraries.

Cargill, Jennifer. "On-line Acquisitions: Use of a Vendor System." *Library Acquisitions: Practice and Theory* 4 (1980): 236-245.

The literature of the '80s contains several articles on the merits of various computerized systems for accomplishing the main tasks of selection, order, receipt, and fund accounting. The methodology of this article set a standard for the many to follow through the decade. With the onset of integrated library systems, the number of articles dealing with specific components may decrease while the number dealing with newly integrated work designs in more comprehensive tech services organizational units increases.

Freedman, Maurice L. "Automation and the Future of Technical Services." *Library Journal* 109 (June 15, 1984): 1197-1203.

A balanced and clear-eyed look at the state of technical services, automation, and their intersection in the 1980s. "Automation is not a panacea, it is a tool," Freedman cautions. It has the potential of making technical services files more accessible to the user. Freedman does not see automation replacing professionals or paraprofessionals, but says it does make possible the redistribution of technical services functions.

Gorman, Michael. "Dealing with Serials: A Sketch of Contextual/ Organizational Response." *Serials Librarian* 10 (1986): 13-18.

After an introductory comment on the chronic underfunding of libraries, Gorman notes the inexorable march of automation with the concomitant changes in the nature of work. Changes in number of serials, price, complexity of publication patterns, and specialization are problems but should not call for a separatist organizational response. Librarians should not be passive about the inconsistency and inefficiency of modern serials publications but should be more militant.

EDUCATION

Battin, Patricia. "Developing University and Research Library Professionals: A Director's Perspective." *American Libraries* 14 (January 1983): 22-25.

Battin's thoughts were directed toward education and qualifications for research librarians, but are generalizable. She says talent — in particular analytical and problem-solving abilities — is more important than credentials in hiring entry-level professionals. She also stresses the importance of managerial skills and objects to the continued emphasis on specialization.

Hill, Janet Swan. "Wanted Good Catalogers." *American Libraries* 16 (November 1985): 728-730.

Sanders, Thomas R. "The Cataloger Crisis: Another View." *American Libraries* 17 (May 1986): 310.

Hill discusses possible reasons for the decrease in numbers and qualifications of applicants for cataloging positions. Contributing factors — such as the women's movement, attractive opportunities in special and corporate libraries, education, and a negative image imparted by library schools — are discussed. Sanders cites the demands of faculty status and the lack of counseling in some library schools as additional explanations.

Hunt, David Marshall and Carol Michael. "Mentorship: A Career Training and Development Tool." Reprinted in *Journal of Library Administration* 5 (Spring 1984): 77-95.

This valuable article surveys mentorship as a training and development tool. Their discussion includes models, frameworks, contexts, characteristics, stages, and a summary of research issues. It is heartening to see ALA's OLPR begin a mentor-type program with its new Librarian Career Resource Network. In general, the column "Worth Repeating from the Management Literature" facilitates scholarly discourse between the two literatures.

Libbey, Maurice C., Guest Editor. "Education for Technical Services" (Special Issue). *Illinois Libraries* 67 (May 1985): 431-496.

In this special issue, practicing librarians, library educators, and former librarians now employed in the commercial sector present opinions, experiences, and research about both formal and informal education for technical services positions. The twenty articles are divided into sections on history, acquisitions, cataloging, serials, media, automation, management, and beyond the library.

Veaner, Allen B. "Technical Services Research Needs for the 1990's." *Library Resources & Technical Services* 27 (April/June 1983): 199-210.

After enumerating factors that support the need for technical services research, Veaner looks at the evolution of research in a changing environment. He defines thirteen specific areas where research can be particularly beneficial: (1) high cost of technical services; (2) costs and values of bibliographic integrity of the catalog; (3) format, extent, and accuracy of bibliographic data; (4) preparation for a new cataloging code; (5) online subject access; (6) acquisitions; (7) integrated, computerized serials control system; (8) universal technical processing terminal; (9) data storage devices; (10) robots and artificial intelligence; (11) commercial technical processing; (12) bibliographic instruction; and (13) human relations, organization, and management issues.

White, Herbert S. "Defining Basic Competencies." *American Libraries* 14 (September 1983): 519-525.

Librarians need to learn to distinguish between education and training, White says, and to decide how much of the latter we are willing to do on the job. His example: "We somehow expect to hire people at 9 a.m., send through personnel indoctrination, and turn them loose on the backlog at 10 a.m." He warns against excessive pragmatism in defining basic competencies and urges prospective employers to look for "potential and intellectual abilities" rather than "immediately useful skills."

MANAGING EXTERNAL CONSTITUENTS

Astle, Deana and Charles Hamaker. "Pricing by Geography: British Journal Pricing 1986, Including Development in Other Countries." *Library Acquisitions: Practice and Theory* 10 (1986): 165-181.

Astle and Hamaker report on the amelioration of price discrimination against American libraries by British publishers. The differential from domestic U.K. and others overseas has diminished by over 40% since the 1984 conference "Learned Journal Pricing and Buying Round." Librarians in the next decade need to continue to make publishers adhere to fair and equitable journal pricing.

Cargill, Jennifer. "Today's Primary Issue—Pricing and Costs of Library Materials: A Conference Report." *Library Acquisitions: Practice & Theory* 10 (1986): 227-228.

The presentation at this conference included: Kent Hendrickson on "Pricing from Three Perspectives: The Publisher, the Wholesaler, and the Library" which focused on a history of pricing policies and the anticipated effect in the decade of the 1980s. Cargill discussed cost savings inside the library from different order mechanisms in "The Approval Connection: Pricing the Ordering Alternatives"; Leonard Schrift predicted a reduction in the number of vendors in the next decade in "Truth in Vendors—Pricing of Monographs, Foreign and Domestic"; Dana Alessi, "Books Across the Waters: An Examination of Foreign Monographic Pricing," focused on the British net book pricing agreement; and in "Mountains and Molehills: How University Presses Determine Book Prices and How Those Prices Relate to Library Budgets," George Bauer talked about price recovery for university presses. Other presentations were "Acquisition Cost: How the Selection of a Purchasing Source Affects the Costs of Processing Materials" by Edna Laughrey whose study showed that using jobbers was beneficial. Christian Boissonnas covered British monograph and serials buying with "Differential Pricing of Monographs and Serials." Kit Kennedy spoke on "The Cost of Global Serials: The Vendor's Perspective" with James T. Stephens talking about "The Library's Cost and the Vendor's Price for Serials." Leonard Clark discussed "Materials Costs and Collection Development" on the effects of pricing on subject selection.

Joyce, Patrick and Thomas E. Merz. "Price Discrimination in Academic Journals." *Library Quarterly* 65 (1985): 273-283.

Joyce and Merz analyze price discrimination for 89 of the "best" academic journals, comparing 1974 prices with 1984 ones. Not only had price discrimination risen markedly from 58.4% to 74.2%, but discrimination had spread among disciplines and publishers. In the next decade, librarians must carry on rigorous relationships with publishers in order to contain the over 1000% abuses in price discrimination.

Loe, Mary H. "Thor Tax Ruling After 5 Years: Its Effect on Publishing and Libraries." *Library Acquisitions: Practice & Theory* 10 (1986): 203-218.

The impact of the Thor Power decision has been to reduce initial press runs by 23% and to put many books out of print within a year. Over 60% of publishers now destroy more books because remaindering has ceased to be an option. Loe urges one more battle against the IRS decision to provide special tax treatment for the publishers' special situation, for a country's laws should not destroy its cultural, scientific, and intellectual heritage.

Naisbitt, John. *Megatrends: Ten New Directions Transforming Our Lives*. New York: Warner, 1982.

Of Naisbitt's ten new directions, the most influential for the library world is the projected shift from an industrial society to an information society in which knowledge is the critical ingredient and librarians are valued professionals. Naisbitt's "knowledge theory of value" should not be news to librarians. Issues of education mismatch, literacy, and computer acuity pose a trenchant challenge for both academic and public library managers.

Paul, Huibert. "Are Subscription Agents Worth Their Keep?" *The Serials Librarian* 7 (1982): 31-41.

Paul cites lack of cooperation from publishers to agents, increasing capacity of publisher to invoice, labor-generating agent practices such as lack of multiple year subscriptions, labor-generating renewal lists, cryptic billing, lack of specific knowledge in billing, and libraries' proclivity for more detailed fund accounting. For financial issues, Paul condenses the argument to whether the cost of check writing is greater than the service charge. Some conclusions revolve around the library budget, exclusive of greater costs to universities and states.

Reid, Marion T. and Scott R. Bullard. "Report on the Business of Acquisitions Preconference." *Library Acquisitions: Practice and Theory* 9 (1985): 283-295.

The title of this preconference for librarians new to acquisitions hammered home the primary concern of the 1980s—business aspects. Keynoter Thomas W. Leonhardt spoke to the roles of acquisitions librarians, booksellers, and book distributors in "The Role and Purpose of Library Acquisitions." In a series of breakout sessions Joan Mancell talked about buying special formats; Sharon Bonk discussed standing order acquisitions; Lorenzo A. Zuegner discoursed on financial management; Edna Laughrey defined firm orders; Linda Pletzke remarked on out-of-print buying; John Reidelbach reviewed approval plans; and Patrick Ashley shared thoughts on gifts. From the publisher's perspective Gary Facente provided an overview of publishing while a publisher panel of Kathleen Ketterman, Ellen Ferber, Catherine Flanagan, and Doris Bass provided additional understanding of publishing practices. Marion Reid talked about utilizing bookseller services. John Secor commented on the search for entrepreneurism in the library world. A bookseller panel with Bent Andersen, Edward Lockman, and Jack Walsdorf answered probing questions from moderator Jennifer Cargill. In "Future Trends in Publishing, Bookselling, and Acquisitions," Susan Harrison predicted uploading of manuscripts to publishers with demand printing of monographs, increasing online transmission of orders to jobbers, and the triumph of optical disk storage as the medium of the 1980s and 1990s.

Strauch, Katrina. "Issues in Book and Serials Acquisitions." *Library Acquisitions: Practice and Theory* 9 (1985): 1-78.

Karen Hitchcock-Mort talked about annual collection planning; Steve Johnson described an effective rush process; Hunter Kevil discussed the philosophy of an approval plan for a smaller library; Martin Faigel addressed collection evaluation; Pam Cenzer contemplated decentralizing acquisitions; and Craig Deitle and Brian Leonard described the history of *Books in Print*. Helen Reed noted the impact of electronic publishing; John Ryland reviewed its ramifications on collection development; Marcia Tuttle described magazine fulfillment centers; Sharon Bonk spoke about evaluating serials agents; and Leonard Schrift updated the Thor Power Tool Supreme Court ruling's effects. A panel of book and serials vendors — Nancy Rodgers, Craig Flansburg, John Secor, Warren Eisenberg, Ed Lockman, and Michael Markwith — covered the topic "Truth in Vending."

Tuttle, Marcia. "Can Subscription Agents Survive?" *Canadian Library Journal* 42 (1985): 259-264.

Tuttle describes the evolution of subscription agents through more aggressive automated services and improved communications. She outlines the role of magazine fulfillment centers, predicts a struggle between fulfillment centers and subscription agencies for control of electronic publishing, and muses on the potentially vanishing role of the librarian. She lauds the communication and cooperation fostered by the U.K. Serials Group and predicts a similar success for the North American Serials Interest Group.

MANAGEMENT TECHNIQUES

Anderson, A. J. "How Do You Manage?" *Library Journal*.

This regular column in *Library Journal* aims to make readers part of the problem and part of the solution. The series consists of short narrative sketches describing typical incidents in library management. Anderson writes the incidents; critiques and analyses are written by practitioners. Personnel, policy, external relationships, and operating procedures in all types of libraries are covered in the series. Anderson's column provides further insights on management problems.

Childers, Thomas, Issue Editor. "Information Organizations: Management Perspectives for the 80's." *Drexel Library Quarterly* 17 *(Spring 1981 issue)*.

In a look at management issues that affect the "information field" (and particularly libraries), the papers draw out of the general and library management literature. Topics include "Human Relations in Management During Periods of Economic Uncertainty," "Organizational Effectiveness in Libraries," and "Organization Structure and the Effectiveness of Information Organizations." Decidedly academic in tone, and lacking in the immediacy of some other articles cited here, these papers nevertheless bring the larger management perspective to library issues.

Crowe, William J. "Zero-Base Budgeting for Libraries: A Second Look." *College and Research Libraries* (January 1982): 47-50.

Zero-base budgeting was an important concept in the management literature of the 1970s. Crowe says that while zero-base budgeting in its pure form may be difficult to apply in libraries, the adoption of zero-base budgeting allows for the involvement of middle managers in the planning and budgeting process.

Darling, John R. and E. Dale Cluff. "Social Styles and the Art of Managing Up." *Journal of Academic Librarianship* 12 (January 1987): 350-355.

Much has been written in the general management literature and in library literature about managing subordinates. This article addresses the less-documented problem of influencing administrators (managing up). The authors describe four social styles and suggest that an understanding of one's own social style and that of one's boss can promote organizational effectiveness through the use of "style flex."

Davis, Peter. "Libraries at the Turning Point: Issues in Proactive Planning." *Journal of Library Administration* 1 (Summer 1980): 11:24.

At the beginning of the decade, Davis examines the environment of the large research library and suggests that strategic planning and implementation of its results are needed if the library is to do anymore than muddle through the 1980s. Librarians are only beginning to come to terms with many of the issues Davis raises. The insights offered by this article should be stimulating for library administrators for the next decade as well.

Drucker, Peter F. *Managing in Turbulent Times* New York: Harper & Row, 1980.

Peter Drucker seems to be quoted in the literature of librarianship more than any other management writer. This book is aimed at managers both in the public and private sectors. Drucker says that a period of turbulence – of radical change in the worldwide population structure and economy as well as in technology – began "some time during the 1970's." Turbulence calls for leadership in the development of strategies not only to cope with rapid change but also to see the opportunities that change may create.

Estabrook, Leigh. "Productivity, Profit, and Libraries." *Library Journal* 106 (July 1981): 1377-1380.

Economic trends that will have major impact on libraries are discussed. The author emphasizes the shift from an industrial to a service-based economy, efforts to increase productivity by adoption of new technology, and the concept of ownership of information. Effects on libraries include an increased emphasis on productivity with a corresponding devaluing of expertise, a tendency to allow certain population to remain unserved, and the mounting controversy over ownership of information.

Georgi, Charlotte and Robert Bellanti, Guest Editors. "Excellence in Library Management." *Journal of Library Administration* 6 (1982): 1-71.

This volume consists of papers presented at the Tenth Annual Workshop on Management for Librarians sponsored by the Southern California chapter of SLA. Taking its theme from the management catchword of the 1980s, the papers speak to ways that excellence can be fostered and maintained in libraries. Offerings include two papers each on "Managing a Special Library," "Managing a Public Library," and "Managing an Academic Library." The final paper, by John J. McDonough, "Power and Human Relations at Work," presents a framework for dealing with competition, power, and politics within the workplace.

Holley, Robert P. "Priority as a Factor in Technical Processing." *Journal of Academic Librarianship* 9 (January 1984): 345-348.

Holley defines a priority system and suggests factors for choosing appropriate processing priorities for a particular library. Internal factors considered include: (1) priority by chronological sequence; (2) influence of organizational structure; (3) priority by personal choice; (4) priority of format; (5) influence of acquisition type; (6) influence of patron; and (7) influence of librarians' judgment. In addition, external factors, such as shared cataloging, the influence of the Library of Congress, and the influence of machine-readable data, come into play with assigning priority.

Malinconico, S. Michael. "Managing Organizational Culture." *Library Journal* 109 (April 15, 1984): 791-793.

One of Malinconico's "Technology, Change and People" columns. He presents the theory of organizational culture with OCLC and AT&T as examples. In managing cultural change, three elements are important: mutual trust, clear goals, and timing and training for change. The closing of Berkeley's card catalog is given as an example of how change can be managed positively.

Martin, Murray S., Editor. "Financial Planning for Libraries." *Journal of Library Administration* 3 (1982): 1-131.

In "Issues in the Financial Management of Research Libraries," Duane E. Webster proposes that libraries need to develop new campus partnerships and better understandings of their role and strength within the institution. In "Financial Planning Needs of Publicly-Supported Academic Libraries in the 1980s: Politics as Usual," Edward R. Johnson surveys fifty-five libraries to determine their expectations of the future and their responses to a perceived need for greater funding. In "Planning and Finance: A Strategic Level Model," Jerome Yavarkovsky describes a strategic level model of the university library to support forecasting, budgeting, and cost accounting. In "Academic Library Decision Support Systems," Michael Bommer and Ronald Chorba propose the development of an electronic decision support system. In "Returning to the Unified Theory of Budgeting: An Umbrella Concept for Public Libraries," Harold R. Jenkins outlines essential management attitudes, operational principles and budgetary strategies for public libraries. In "Salary Planning," Paul M. Gherman recommends developing algorithms to project costs for personnel for the changing nature of the library. In "Interlibrary Loan and Resource Sharing: New Approaches," Noelene P. Martin argues that a revolutionized interlibrary loan service forces collection development librarians to rethink organizational function and financial status. In "Financial Planning for Collection Management," Frederick C. Lynden urges communication about financial, economic, political, environmental, and educational factors in justifying the materials budget. In "Budgeting for and Controlling the Cost of *Other* In-Library Expenditures: The Distant Relative in the Budgetary Process," Sherman Hayes notes that the advent of computerization requires library managers to pay closer attention to this growing part of the budget.

McClure, Charles R., Guest Editor. "Planning for Library Services: A Guide to Utilizing Planning Methods for Library Management." *Journal of Library Administration* 2 (1981): 1-250.

This special issue contains fifteen articles on planning for academic, public, school, and special libraries. Staffing for planning, pitfalls of planning, training for planning, psychology of planning, the literature of planning, the national aspects of planning, and other topics are covered.

Peters, Thomas J. and Robert H. Waterman. *In Search of Excellence: Lessons from American's Best-Run Companies*. New York: Harper & Row, 1982.

This study of sixty-two successful United States companies has some interesting implications for librarians. Peters' chapters "Managing Ambiguity and Paradox" and "A Bias for Action" both offer useful counsel. Peters' point that excellent companies are learning organizations (a good definition for a library) is particularly heartening. In *A Passion for Excellence: The Leadership Difference* (New York: Random House, 1985), a less successful sequel, Tom Peters and Nancy Austin remind us that management is an art, not a science. Managing by walking around is a technique practiced by many technical services librarians, whose own job expertise makes perambulation worthwhile. Obsession with quality, a frequent area of disagreement between administration and library workers, receives validation. Not much library literature exists on the elusive topic of leadership, but many of the concrete examples cited here provide workable leadership styles.

Valentine, Phyllis A. "Increasing Production in Cataloging while Decreasing Cost." *Technicalities* 4 (July 1984): 10-13.

Responding to reduced funding, the cataloging department of The University of Michigan Library scrutinized both its process and its product. Changes included establishment of an automated processing unit, utilizing support personnel for duties previously assigned to professionals, and post-receipt authority checking. Resultant increases in cataloging production and decreases in the staff budget are documented.

PERSONNEL

Conroy, Barbara. "The Human Element: Staff Development in the Electronic Library." *Drexel Library Quarterly* 17 (Fall 1981): 91-106.

As libraries move from the initiation to the expansion stage of automation, appropriate staff development efforts are required to enable library personnel to adapt to the demands of the new technology and to assure the efficient functioning of the library as a whole. Training needs of all levels of staff must be taken into account as the electronic library develops.

Euster, Joanne R. "Leaders and Managers: Literature Review Synthesis and a New Conceptual Framework." *Journal of Library Administration* 5 (1984): 45-61.

Library administrators are charged with failure in attempts to solve societal information problems and in utilizing innovative managerial techniques to administer the library. Four descriptions of leadership are supplied. Mintzberg's threefold definition and his ten managerial roles are surveyed. Euster suggests further research into leader behavior, distribution of leadership roles, and a leader's relationship to the parent organization.

Evans, G. Edward and Bendik Rugaas. "Another Look at Performance Appraisal in Libraries." *Journal of Library Administration* 3 (1982): 61-69.

The authors provide a comprehensive list of expectations from the performance evaluations but they question the basic tenet — the assumption that appraisal leads to better performance. Evans' CLR funded sojourn in Scandinavian libraries where performance evaluations are unknown and his survey in Great Britain where a less structured approach is used are related.

Horny, Karen L. "Quality Work, Quality Control in Technical Services." *Journal of Academic Librarianship* 11 (September 1985): 206-210.

The author views the effects of automation on the persistent dilemma of quality versus productivity in technical services, particularly processing. Key considerations in quality control include accepted bibliographic standards, users' needs, access to records, and human factors. New skills required of both managers and staff, as well as the benefits of improved error detection and authority control, are discussed.

LAMA/PAS Staff Development Committee. "Staff Development Column." *Library Administration & Management*, passim.

The pithy annotations of useful articles on a variety of management topics make this continuing feature extremely worthwhile. The articles reviewed are drawn from a variety of journals in management, librarianship, and systems. Change, the implementation of automation, staff education, training, personnel issues, and a variety of other topics fall within the purview of this column.

Leung, Shirley W. "Coping with Stress: A Technical Services Perspective." *Journal of Library Administration* 5 (1984): 1-19.

Leung identifies common stressors which affect technical services librarians. Job-related factors, interpersonal difficulties, and organizational stressors are discussed with measures which may serve to diminish stress.

Lipow, Anne G. "Thawing Staff Attitudes about a 'Frozen' Catalog." *Library Journal* 106 (March 1981): 618-722.

When the decision was made to close the card catalog at the University of California, Berkeley, the Catalog Instruction Group was charged with public relations, user information, and staff instruction. The author stresses the importance of staff involvement at all levels, broad-based decision-making, keeping everyone informed, allowing mistakes, emphasizing humor, and fostering creativity.

Malinconico, S. Michael. "People and Machines: Changing Relationships?" *Library Journal* 108 (December 1, 1983): 2222-2224.

Another in Malinconico's "Technology, Change, and People" columns (all of them are worth reading: the two singled out are particularly relevant). Contrary to expectations, Malinconico says, the new information technologies have not had the liberating effects on workers that was expected of them, but often have resulted in the same feelings of alienation experienced by workers in mass production jobs. Malinconico reasons that automation is still in a mechanized phase, but the possibility will exist for workers to enjoy more freedom and responsibility.

McKinley, Margaret M. "Serials Departments: Doomed to Extinction?" *The Serials Librarian* 5 (1980): 15-24.

Organizing to accomplish serials objectives has been a recurrent subject of discussion in the 1980s. McKinley here opens the decade's discourse with a sage comment on the importance of good communications, no matter how serials may be organized. Her emphasis on the motivated and experienced serials specialist as an expert communicator within and across organizational boundaries remains timely in the face of further changes.

ROLE OF TECH SERVICES IN THE LIBRARY

Bishoff, Lizbeth, Guest Editor. "Technical Services in the Small Library." *Library Resources & Technical Services* 29 (April/June 1985): 118-171.

Small libraries, both public and college, are a neglected topic in the tech services literature. This issue of *LRTS* attempts to remedy this deficiency. Articles treat all facets of technical services—management issues of automation, serials control, bibliographic control, collection development and preservation—as applied to the small library. The authors address not only the current state of tech services but also future directions.

Bousfield, Wendy. "Boundary Spanners and Serials Deselection." *Serials Librarian* 10 (1986): 23-31.

In a time when economic factors are forcing many libraries to consider seriously engaging in a serials deselection project, Bousfield recognizes the economic necessity for such projects but reminds librarians that cancellations reduce the library's ability to support scholarship. The library subject specialist acts to educate faculty in alternative methods for obtaining information.

Dwyer, James R. "The Effect of Closed Catalogs on Public Access." *Library Resources & Technical Services* 25 (April/June 1981): 186-195.

This catalog use study at the University of Oregon indicates that users resist searching catalogs that require multiple lookups. Based on surveys, Dwyer believes that this dissatisfaction includes closed catalogs with COM supplements, divided catalogs, and separate catalogs for different classification schemes. Urgency in retrospective conversion projects is stressed.

Gorman, Michael. "Thinking the Thinkable: A Synergetic Profession." *American Libraries* 13 (July/August 1982): 473-474.

In his final regular column for *American Libraries,* Gorman focuses on the potential and challenge of the online catalog. Contrasting online catalogs with traditional ones, he views the planning stages and the inevitable changes in both public services and technical services areas, which will accompany implementation of an online system. The column closes with a challenge to the profession to shape the future with cooperation and plurality.

Holley, Robert P. "The Future of Catalogers and Cataloging." *Journal of Academic Librarianship* 7 (May 1981): 90-93.

Holley describes changes in the cataloging department's philosophy and functioning that have resulted from budgetary limitations. He explains ways in which both financial considerations and the impact of automation have altered the relationship of the cataloging department to the whole library community. Utilizing his analysis of present trends as a springboard to predictions for the future, the author sees catalogers falling into four possible categories: (1) those at Library of Congress; (2) those in large research libraries; (3) those in managerial roles; and (4) those in integrated scholar-librarian special subject positions.

Horny, Karen L. "New Turns for a New Century: Library Services in an Information Age." *Library Resources & Technical Services* 31 (January/March 1987): 6-11.

On the occasion of RTSD's thirtieth birthday, Horny speculated on what the library of 2006 might be like. She predicts "online catalog access to the full range of library collections, nationwide and beyond, regardless of the format in which the text resides." Increasingly, "resources will be accessed but not owned by libraries." Books will continue to exist but journals and other "shorter documents" will be almost entirely in an electronic format. The librarian's role in organizing "access to textual resources" will remain vital.

Johnson, Millard F. "After the Online Catalog: A Call for Active Librarianship." *American Libraries* 13 (April 1982): 235-242.

Johnson asserts that today's passive library is a warehouse that makes poor use of its librarians and that focuses on information in a physical package. The advent of new library technology makes possible active librarianship with the goal of providing the patron with all the information needed. This article outlines the difference between the two approaches to librarianship.

McClure, Charles R. "Academic Librarians, Information Sources and Shared Decision Making." *Journal of Academic Librarianship* 6 (1980): 9-15.

One conclusion of this article is that technical services librarians are relatively information-poor. Both administrators and public services librarians contact more information sources than do technical services librarians. Information-rich individuals were always identified as being involved in decision-making. McClure suggests that people seek information to decrease uncertainty and that technical services librarians might have less need for information contact.

McCombs, Gillian. "Public and Technical Services: Disappearing Barriers." *Wilson Library Bulletin* 61 (November 1986): 25-28.

Technical services, the author insists, should be evaluated in light of their ability to provide the patron with needed information. The changing role of the cataloger, the opportunity of the online catalog, and the difficulty of offering online authority control and syndetic references are major topics for discussion. Calling for an end to traditional crossfire between reference librarians and catalogers, McCombs emphasizes the need for future librarians to embrace an integrated or Renaissance approach.

Shaughnessy, Thomas W. "Technology and the Structure of Libraries." *Libri* 32 (1982): 149-155.

A theoretical paper which argues that "library structures have not sufficiently changed to accommodate new technologies, and that this has resulted in poor utilization of staff and user frustration." Libraries are still structured according to the two main types of input they receive: resources (technical services) and users (public services). Although Shaughnessy does not propose a particular structure, he states that any model must recognize that the new information technologies are changing the nature of both the input and the output of libraries, and that an opportunity exists for new organizational structures.

Stevenson, Gordon and Sally Stevenson, Editors. "Reference Services and Technical Services: Interaction in Library Practice." *The Reference Librarian* 9 (Fall/Winter 1983): 3-176.

In this special issue, librarians discuss various facets of the relationship between public services and technical services. Wayne Wiegand provides the historical background, and Gordon Stevenson offers an overview, "Current Issues in Technical Services." Pauline Cochrane, Michael Gorman, and Larry Earl Bone comment on various organizational arrangements. A section on document description contains articles on topics ranging from the impact of AACR2 at Harvard to interlibrary loan and access to serials collections. A section entitled "Subject Organization and Access" consists of five articles on subject access or classification schemes.